PRAISE FOR *WINNING AT SOCIAL CUSTOMER CARE*

"Finally - a book on social customer care that is both applicable and uniquely insightful! Dan Gingiss is a master of spelling out how your brand can win in the often-confused space of social customer care. Full of case studies and gushing with his own unique expertise and experience in the space, this is one book that will propel your brand to greatness in social." – Neal Schaffer, author of *Maximize Your Social*

"The thing about customer experience is that your customers will have experiences on their own terms. Those experiences add up to their interpretation of your brand, product and service. Social care is about meeting customers in the channels they use. Gone are the days of forcing them to engage with companies simply because that's the investment that was made. Here Dan Gingiss shares how social can make companies more human and engaged to deliver better experiences, build relationships, and earn loyalty." – Brian Solis, leading digital analyst, anthropologist, futurist and author of *X: The Experience Meets Design*

This isn't just any book, it's a handbook for creating the best human experiences for your customers. Dan Gingiss walked the walk by making the book itself an experience. Bravo!! – Bryan Kramer, TED Speaker, USA Today Best-Selling Author, Consultant

"The business world has changed forever and if you are not proactive, your brand is going to be history. Gingiss details exactly how to stay significantly ahead of the pack. *Winning at Social Customer Care* couldn't be more timely and relevant. Every management team needs to read and create a social media strategy plan around the "8 Steps to Winning at Social Customer Care." – John R. DiJulius III, author of *The Customer Service Revolution*

"Dan Gingiss is the real deal, having run Social Customer Care for two major brands. Through his wisdom, experience and research, he teaches us one of today's most powerful and important business strategies. So, don't just read this book. Use it to implement and enhance your Social Customer Care program… before your competition does!" – Shep Hyken, customer service expert and *New York Times* best-selling author of *The Amazement Revolut*

WINNING AT SOCIAL
CUSTOMER CARE

WINNING AT SOCIAL CUSTOMER CARE

HOW TOP BRANDS CREATE ENGAGING EXPERIENCES ON SOCIAL MEDIA

Dan Gingiss

Foreword by Jay Baer

ISBN: 1542732387
ISBN 13: 9781542732383
Library of Congress Control Number: 2017901244
CreateSpace Independent Publishing Platform
North Charleston, South Carolina

For Jodi, Mark, and Samantha

CONTENTS

Foreword · i

Introduction· ·v

1 Start With A Great Customer Experience · · · · · · · · · · · · · · · · · · · 1
   What is Customer Experience?
   How is Customer Experience Measured?
   Why is Customer Experience Important?
   Customer Experience Examples
   User Experience

2 Social Media's Role in Customer Experience · · · · · · · · · · · · · · · ·16
   What Gets Shared?
   Offline Can Come Online at Any Time
   What You Need to Do
   Creating a "Wow" Moment

3 Why Social Customer Care ·27
   Responding on Social Media
   Social Customer Care by the Numbers
   The "Wow" Moment Revisited
   What Do I Need to Do?
   The "8 Steps to Winning at Social Customer Care"

4 Philosophy (Winning at Social Customer Care Step #1)· · · · · · · · · 40
   Philosophy Examples

5   Technology (Winning at Social Customer Care Step #2) · · · · · · · · · ·49
        What Is It?
        What Do You Need to Think About?
        Three Different Types of Technology
        Which Is the Best Solution for You?

6   Team Selection (Winning at Social Customer Care Step #3) · · · · · · ·59
        What Do You Need to Look For?
        Internal or External?
        Organizational Structure
        Incentive Structures
        Scaling

7   Training (Winning at Social Customer Care Step #4) · · · · · · · · · · ·72
        Your Core Business
        Most Frequent Inquiry Types
        Internal Systems and Policies
        Social Media Platforms
        Community Management
        Public Customer Service

8   Process (Winning at Social Customer Care Step #5) · · · · · · · · · · · ·83
        What Is It?
        When to Take Discussions Off-Channel
        Escalation Procedures
        What to Do in a Crisis
        Empowering the Team
        Responding to Compliments
        Dealing With Trolls
        Response Time
        Platform-Specific Decisions
        Proactive Customer Care

9   Reporting (Winning at Social Customer Care Step #6) · · · · · · · · · ·103
        Key Performance Indicators

10   Integration With the Core Business
        (Winning at Social Customer Care Step #7) · · · · · · · · · · · · · ·114

What Is It?
Voice of the Customer
Feedback Loop
Other Integration Points

11   Integration With CRM
     (Winning at Social Customer Care Step #8) · · · · · · · · · · · · ·122
     What Is It?
     Three Facets of CRM Integration
     Personalization

12   The Proliferation of Messaging Apps ·128
     Bots

13   Other Social Customer Care Channels ·136
     Communities
     Ratings and Reviews Sites

14   The Future of Social Customer Care ·141
     Marketing Your Customer Service
     What's Next

Acknowledgements ·145
Photos and Charts ·147
Notes ·149
Index ·161
About the Author ·169

FOREWORD

Eventually, your competitors will mimic everything you do well. They'll copy your products. They'll ape your website copy. They'll match or beat your prices. And they'll go after your best employees and customers. They. Just. Will.

But there's one thing your competition cannot take from you. The one element of your business that is defensible and protectable is if you genuinely provide a better customer experience. Companies that care more about their customers' satisfaction eventually win market share.

Put simply, customer experience is how you make your customers feel about you. And those feelings are all about expectations. When you exceed them, you deliver a "great customer experience." And when you fall short of expectations it results in a "terrible customer experience." And customer experience correlates with revenue. In fact, according to the research firm Walker, by 2020, customer experience will be more important than price in most business-to-business buying decisions.

As you'll learn in these pages, one of the very best ways to exceed expectations - thereby creating a great customer experience and triggering positive feelings - is through social customer care.

This is true for three reasons:

First, more and more of your customers are using social media to interact with your business. This flood from offline to online interactions will not abate. And it benefits both parties: customers often get demonstrably better service in social media; and for most businesses it is less expensive to provide service on those platforms, versus phone, email and other legacy channels.

Second, most of your competitors are unprepared for this change. Of course, there are some terrific examples of companies embracing social care and using it as a competitive differentiator. My good friend Dan Gingiss chronicles many of them in this book, and he himself has led transformative social care programs that are near-mythical in the industry. But in general, the fact that you are reading this book puts you FAR ahead of most of your competitors. Now is the time to outflank them, before they realize just how much impact social care will have on company success.

And third, because so many companies are still napping on this trend, consumers themselves don't expect a whole lot. Customer experience is about exceeding expectations, and it's still viable to do just that in social care without heroic measures. As a whole, consumers aren't jaded and cynical about customer service in social media the way they largely are about customer service via phone and email (not to mention postal mail and fax). With relative ease, you can still use social care to turn frustrated customers into volunteer marketers, and doing so only doubles-down on the revenue impact of these programs.

This is not a book that is important. This is a book that is existentially important. It doesn't matter if other companies in your industry are good at this yet. Eventually, they will be because customers will demand it; the same way customers demanded we use email and build websites and offer free shipping and stay open 24 hours. And until then, it's actually great news if your competitors haven't fully embraced social care. It gives you the opportunity to make it a major differentiator for your business. After all, without great customer service, great marketing is a waste of time and money.

Every day, companies are realizing that social care adds up. Comcast had one of the earliest social care programs in the world, but then let it go mostly dormant. Recently, they had a reawakening to the manifest business potential of being great at customer service via social media, and increased their social care team from 13 people to nearly 400! Why? Because it's faster, and customers are happier when they use social to get help.

You'll be happier too, when you finish this book. Because in *Winning at Social Customer Care*, Dan Gingiss gives you PRECISELY what you need to do this well, and do this right.

I know Dan. I've worked with Dan. Dan was the star of my own book on this topic. And I've read this book. And I can tell you that nowhere will you find a more practical, comprehensive guide to making social customer care a competitive advantage. This is the kind of book that you don't read once, you read it forever. You'll keep it on your desk as a reference, flipping back to specific ideas and recommendations and statistics, steadily building your own social care successes.

You'll be inspired, too. Not just by Dan and his passion for the subject, but by the dozens of other social care pioneers whose insights, ideas, and experiences are included here. You'll feel their pain and celebrate their triumphs.

Together, the pros included in *Winning at Social Customer Care* and you, the readers, are a community. We are a team. We know that a profound shift is occurring in business that will redefine how companies interact with their customers, and as a result, change who wins and who loses in every industry. We also know that this shift remains unseen by many people, giving us a rare opportunity to capitalize on competitors' skepticism and aversion to change.

Social customer care is our opportunity to disrupt, lead, and win. Dan Gingiss gives us the playbook for what to do, how to do it, and why it works.

Winning at Social Customer Care is our secret weapon. Turn the page, and let's activate it.

Jay Baer
President of Convince & Convert and author of *Hug Your Haters: How to Embrace Complaints and Keep Your Customers*

January, 2017

INTRODUCTION

S ome things just can't be taught.

I found my first job after college at The Danbury Mint – a high-end collectibles company selling porcelain dolls, figurines, sports memorabilia and the like – by seeing a newspaper advertisement before anyone else. As I was putting the finishing touches on an issue of *The Daily Pennsylvanian*, the student newspaper of the University of Pennsylvania, I noticed an ad that promised to "teach you everything you need to know about direct marketing." Knowing very little about marketing, I had a lot to learn.

The company delivered on its promise. At age 22, I was given ownership of several multimillion-dollar product lines and told to develop and execute marketing plans to grow sales. My love for marketing was officially kindled.

But what they didn't teach me – what I sort of already knew but had to experience on my own – was how to deal with an angry customer.

One year during the week of Christmas, a call came through to my desk. I was in the Marketing department, not Customer Service, but the call somehow got to me and I answered it. An elderly lady was on the phone and she was livid. We were ruining her Christmas because the gift that she had bought her grandson had not arrived. It was December 23rd.

As I listened to her talk, it was just instinct that kicked in. I told her that Christmas was not going to be ruined on my account. I didn't have access to the Customer Service system, so I wrote down her name and address and figured out what product she needed from a catalog on my desk. I walked over to our warehouse, which was luckily in the same building, and checked the product off the shelf. I packed it up in a box with plenty of shipping peanuts. Then I personally walked it over to the mailroom and made sure that the package got out the door via Overnight Express – to be delivered on the 24th.

That wasn't in any training manual. I may have even broken a company policy. But that was what my instinct said to do because I wanted to take care of that customer. And you know what? She became a customer for life.

These days, Customer Service – both good and bad – is played out in the open on social media. While there are countless examples of unfortunate gaffes and public relations nightmares on social, that's not what this book is about. This book is about treating your customers right every time, exceeding customer experience expectations, and delivering memorable Customer Service in what I like to call "the world's most public Customer Service channel."

Throughout the book, there will be examples and case studies from top brands that have appeared on my *Focus on Customer Service* podcast. There are big brands, medium-sized brands, and some smaller brands you probably haven't heard of. They are all leading the way in Social Customer Care by creating engaging experiences for their customers.

I have learned so much from the nearly four dozen Customer Service leaders I have interviewed on the podcast, and I can't wait to share those learnings with you. Indeed, the "8 Steps to Winning at Social Customer Care" were designed after combining those insights with my own experience leading Social Customer Care at multiple Fortune 300 companies. So think of this book as the ultimate compilation of best practices.

One leader, Allison Leahy, the director of community at Fitbit, said on the podcast that Customer Service professionals should learn from as many sources as possible.

"Curate some of the best articles, podcasts, philosophies, [and] ideas that you hear as you're exploring Social Customer Care and community management," she said. "If you actually make a little bit of effort to start compiling some of these resources, it can be really, really valuable along the way because as your career advances, you might want to help educate your peers and build your team on a foundation of knowledge."[1]

Indeed, this book does "curate some of the best articles, podcasts, philosophies, [and] ideas" so you don't have to. In fact, all of the quotes in the book are from *Focus on Customer Service* podcast episodes, except for the references to other published works. While you can't teach instinct, you can definitely share best practices.

I am confident that you can achieve the same kind of success enjoyed by the stellar brands featured in this book, no matter your company size, team size, or budget size. Let's get going!

1

Start With A Great Customer Experience

As the world of social media increases in size and scale, it becomes an increasingly bigger part of the overall customer experience (CX). Customers now expect to be able to engage with brands wherever and whenever they want, and a brand's response (or lack thereof) plays a big role in customer satisfaction and loyalty.

Much has been written about customer experience, which won't be rehashed in this book. But it is useful to agree on a simple definition of customer experience, which will guide our discussion about social media's influence.

WHAT IS CUSTOMER EXPERIENCE?

> *Customer Experience is how customers <u>feel</u> about <u>every single interaction</u> with a brand.*

What can we glean from this definition? How customers *feel* is an important piece of the puzzle, because not everyone feels the same way about the same thing. As the old saying goes, "perception is reality," so it's critical that brands truly understand how their customers are interacting with them and what it's actually like to be a customer.

If your customers feel that your mobile app is difficult to navigate, then it's difficult to navigate, regardless of whether your designers or IT department say it's simple. So understanding how your products or services make customers feel will go a long way toward ensuring that your customers end up happy.

Too often brands build experiences that serve their own purposes but neglect to consider how a customer will feel in the middle of it. To alleviate this blind spot, brands should involve their customers in the creation of experiences – both online and offline – to ensure the customer's point of view is understood.

The other important part of this definition is that customer experience includes *every single interaction* that a customer has with a brand. Because so many companies operate in silos, this is something that many brands miss. Let's look at a fictional fast food restaurant as an example.

If I asked you to name the most important part of the customer experience at a fast food restaurant, you might say, "the food." You'd be right in a sense – the quality of the food is a huge contributor to the overall customer experience ("Where do you want to go to lunch?" "To that place with the awful food," said no one ever.) But it's far from the only part, and may not even be the most important, as I'll explain in a moment.

What else is included in the customer experience? Believe it or not, the experience likely starts before the customer even walks into the restaurant – in the parking lot. Finding a place to park is often stressful and time-consuming, and it may put a customer in a bad mood before beginning the meal. (At a more upscale restaurant with a valet, the friendliness – and trustworthiness – of the valet attendant is critical to the experience.)

After entering the restaurant, there are a series of "micro-moments" that contribute to the overall customer experience. These can include:

- Could I read the menu without squinting?
- How long did I have to wait in line?
- Did the cashier welcome me or treat me in a friendly way? Did he or she get my order right?
- How long did I have to wait for my food?
- Was my food delivered at the right temperature? (My dad always likes to say, "I like my hot food hot and my cold food cold.")

- Did they have my favorite beverage available? (Many a Coke vs. Pepsi war is fought in fast food restaurants!)
- Was the temperature of the restaurant comfortable? (Have you ever sat in a restaurant shivering every time someone opens the door?)
- Was my preferred method of payment – debit card, credit card, Apple Pay, Android Pay – accepted?
- Were there enough condiments, napkins, and utensils available? (I've never understood why some restaurants insist on hiding the napkins.)
- And perhaps most importantly to those of us with kids – Was it a cool toy in the kids' meal? (We all know that if the kids aren't happy, neither are we!)

So there's a lot more than just the quality of the food that goes into the customer experience. But wait, there's more! We have only covered the physical experience; what about the digital experience? That introduces questions like:

- Did the restaurant have a website? Could I view the menu in advance? Could I order ahead or make a reservation?
- Did the restaurant have a mobile app?
- Have I seen marketing from the restaurant, and if so, how did that make me feel? Was it intrusive, or effectively targeted at just the right moment? (This is both a digital and physical phenomenon, as anyone who has received an unwanted pizza menu stuffed in their door handle – or an annoying pop-up ad on a website – can attest.)
- What does the restaurant's social media presence look like? Are their posts all promotional vs. helpful or useful? How often do they post? And do they actively engage with customers?

All of the above contribute to how a customer *feels* about a fast-food restaurant brand, because taken together they (hypothetically) encompass *every single interaction* that a customer has had with that brand.

What if you are not operating a restaurant? Chances are your company operates in silos, with different people "owning" different parts of the customer journey. This is especially true at larger companies. Here is another fictional example that could be familiar to any business:

The person who "owns" digital display advertising at a company has Agency A design an ad placement aimed at driving people to purchase a product with a special offer. But when the user clicks on the ad, they get to a landing page – designed by Agency B via the team that "owns" the product's web experience – which contains a different offer from the ad, or which uses colors and fonts that don't look like the same company. Confused, the user decides to open up the brand's mobile app – designed by Agency C via the team that "owns" the mobile app experience – and they don't see any reference to the advertising offer at all (but they do see new colors and fonts). Now frustrated, the user calls Customer Service with some choice words for the agent on the other end, who has no idea what advertisement the person is talking about.

What is the result of this example? The person probably ends up buying from someone else, so the company has spent money and human capital on an advertisement, a telephone call, and two digital experiences that lead to the wrong result.

One more part of the customer experience that we cannot forget about – and which forms the basis for this book – is Customer Service. Many people confuse Customer Service and customer experience. Customer Service is a single interaction, so therefore it is a subset of customer experience, which is a series of interactions.

Getting back to our restaurant example: Scott Wise, owner of more than a dozen Scotty's Brewhouse restaurants in the Midwest, said on a podcast episode that he is "in the business of Customer Service."[2]

What? A guy who owns more than a dozen restaurants isn't in the restaurant business, but rather he's in the Customer Service business? Absolutely, said Wise, adding that if a restaurant has delicious food but terrible service, it fails because it has no customers. But if a restaurant has great food – or even just good food – and outstanding, memorable service, its customers will remain loyal for years to come.

Similarly, when I asked best-selling author and Customer Service expert Shep Hyken if he thinks that all companies are in the Customer Service business today, he replied: "Not just all companies. Everybody who works in the company is in service."[3]

Hyken cited a New Voice Media study which found that U.S. companies are losing $62 billion – with a "b" – every year due to poor Customer Service.[4]

"Now that would indicate to most people that Customer Service is getting worse," he said. "I don't think it is getting worse. I think Customer Service is getting better. What's happened is that customers' expectations are higher than they've ever been. That is outpacing the strides that some of these companies are making."[5]

The bottom line is this: Everything is about the customer. Without customers, there is no business. You must view everything you do through your customers' eyes and make every effort to ensure that each customer's experience is simple, positive, and memorable. And this philosophy should be instilled into every employee, especially those on the "front line" who interact with your customers every day.

Have you ever encountered a cashier at a fast food restaurant who looks at you like you are interrupting their otherwise pleasant day? Maybe that person should be reminded that without those interruptions, he or she doesn't have a job.

"The world has gotten so complacent and okay with good service – not even good, average – it's almost like we think average service nowadays is acceptable," said Wise. "We're like, 'Oh my god, they actually took care of me, they arrived in the right amount time, the food was lukewarm and I got out of here in a decent amount of time, and that was pretty good service.' That wasn't good service, that was average, crappy service. Why would we be okay with that?"[6]

Research shows that fewer and fewer companies and industries are able to compete on price these days, because consumers are demanding a great customer experience as well. Savvy brands have figured out that they don't have to be the lowest-cost provider if their experience is extraordinary.

"You're going to compete on really one of two things. You're either going to compete on price or something else," said Hyken. "That something else is always going to be part of the customer experience ... If they want to experience just the low price and that's the only thing, as soon as that customer finds somewhere else to give them a lower price they're going to do that ... Keep in mind that the customer [who] is loyal to price is never loyal to a company. They're only loyal to the price."[7]

John R. DiJulius III owns The DiJulius Group, a Customer Service consulting firm in Cleveland whose purpose is "to change the world by creating a Customer Service revolution." His book of the same name (*Customer Service Revolution*) explains that the goal is to provide such a great customer experience, that price no longer matters. Specifically, a Customer Service revolution is:

> *"A radical overthrow of conventional business mentality designed to transform what employees and Customers experience. This shift produces a culture that permeates into people's personal lives, at home, and in the community, which in turn provides the business with higher sales, morale, and brand loyalty – making price irrelevant."*[8]

HOW IS CUSTOMER EXPERIENCE MEASURED?

There are a variety of ways to measure customer experience, and to get a complete picture brands should incorporate several of them.

The first way to measure customer experience is to simply ask your customers. Whether this is through traditional customer research like surveys or focus groups, or through user testing of specific experiences, ask and you shall receive feedback.

Another way to measure it is essentially the converse of the first way: let customers come to you, and measure their sentiment. This is also called Voice of the Customer. It can take the form of direct feedback through existing Customer Service channels, ratings and reviews, third-party discussion boards, or social media listening.

Finally, brands can turn to third-party evaluators to measure customer experience. Companies like Forrester and J.D. Power have different proprietary methods for measuring satisfaction, which usually provide objective, quantifiable and actionable results, as well as valuable competitive data. Keep in mind, though, that a brand's goal should not be to win an award or "beat" a survey. The goal should be to provide a best-in-class customer experience, which will in turn lead to positive results in third-party evaluations.

WHY IS CUSTOMER EXPERIENCE IMPORTANT?

Although conceptually most brands understand that providing their customers with a memorable experience is a good thing, some brands still need to be convinced that doing so also leads to positive business results. Thankfully, the research supports this claim.

Forrester looked at the correlation between customer experience and several loyalty metrics – including willingness to consider the company for another purchase, likelihood to recommend it to a friend, and likelihood to switch to a competitor – and found a statistically significant correlation with each of them.[9]

Higher retention rates and more customer referrals lead to more overall usage, which leads to higher revenues. But customer experience also has a positive effect on the other side of the profitability coin, which is cost. It stands to reason that an outstanding customer experience reduces Customer Service inquiries and regulatory fines, both of which can become quite costly to brands doing it wrong.

Forrester took it a step further and "compared five pairs of publicly traded companies where one company in each of the pairs had a significantly higher score than the other in Forrester's Customer Experience Index during the period 2010 to 2015." The firm calculated the compound annual growth rate (CAGR) of each company and found that "the CX leaders in all five pairs of companies outperformed their relative CX laggard counterparts."[10]

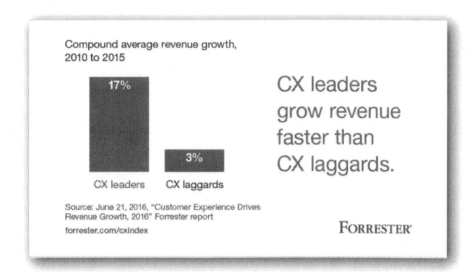

CUSTOMER EXPERIENCE EXAMPLES

Now let's look at some real-life customer experience examples. As you look at the pictures, think about how you might *feel* if you were engaging with this brand. Here's a sign outside of a national fast food restaurant chain:

"Quality service that doesn't cut corners is our recipe." Wow! This is kind of like Scott Wise putting Customer Service above even the quality of the food. What's great about this sign is that is tells the customer – before they even walk in – that the service at this restaurant is going to be great. No doubt the company is creating high expectations which it will need to at least meet if not exceed, but a company is not going to put that sign on the side of its building if it isn't committed to creating a great experience. Do you know which restaurant this is? If you guessed Wendy's, you are right.

Now compare that first sign to this one, which was the *first thing I saw* when I entered a different fast-food restaurant (that will remain nameless):

"We cannot provide any courtesy cups." How does that make you feel? My first instinct was to point out that the sign was actually wrong – it's not that they *cannot* provide any courtesy cups, it's that they *will not*. But more than that, this sign tells me that the restaurant does not have my needs in mind. It is so focused on the bottom line that it is willing to degrade the customer experience just to save a few pennies.

If that's the case with the cups, who knows where else it might be the case? Maybe I'll get less meat on my sandwich, or those tomatoes that should have been thrown out two days ago are still in the cooler. Maybe the bathrooms aren't clean – or the sandwich maker's hands. Grossed out yet? Is that how you want to feel when you're getting ready to order your lunch? I can't imagine what caused this restaurant to believe that putting up this sign was a good idea, but I am sure it wasn't worth it.

How about this sign, found at a local gas station?

"Assistance available when 2 cashiers on duty." This sign makes me laugh every time. So apparently employee scheduling and availability is now *my* problem as the customer? If I drive up and there is only one cashier on duty, I'm just out of luck if I need assistance? What do you think is the very next thing I would do if that scenario occurred? Drive to the next gas station. (As a side note, and this may just be my quirky sense of humor, but I also find myself wondering what happens if there are three cashiers on duty.)

Signs like this are just unnecessary. Even if we give the benefit of the doubt to the owner/operator of the gas station and assume that something that sounds reasonable caused him to make this sign – maybe it's a safety or security issue – it is the wrong message to send to paying customers without context.

You may be thinking that a sign like that lowers customer expectations to the point where the gas station actually has a better chance of meeting or exceeding expectations. After all, if there's only one cashier on duty and I still get assistance, that's a big win, right? I don't think that argument prevails. As the power has shifted from brands to customers in social media, most customers begin with high expectations and are not likely going to be influenced to lower them.

USER EXPERIENCE

According to the International Organization for Standardization, user experience is a "person's perceptions and responses resulting from the use and/or anticipated use of a product, system or service" and is "a consequence of brand image, presentation, functionality, system performance, interactive behaviour and assistive capabilities of the interactive system."[11] User experience is a subset of customer experience, but it is a critical piece. While the term is often used in relation to digital experience (ease of navigation, form fields that allow for quick data entry, accessibility options, etc.), it also has applications in the physical world.

It is important to note that not every user experiences a product in the same way. For example, iPhone users of a certain age sometimes set the font so large that to me it looks like only four or five words fit on the screen. But that's because Apple – which is known for creating an unbeatable user experience – understood that older eyes need larger font sizes, and that the ability to choose one's own font size allows the user to personalize his or her experience.

Back to the physical world: Consider this garbage receptacle found at a pastry shop in a high-end Las Vegas strip hotel:

After my wife and I enjoyed our coffee and muffins, I went to put away my tray and noticed how large the hole was in the countertop. It was remarkable because I am so used to tiny receptacles that only fit a coffee cup. The remnants of our breakfast slid easily off the tray into the garbage. On a whim I decided to see if the tray would fall in as well:

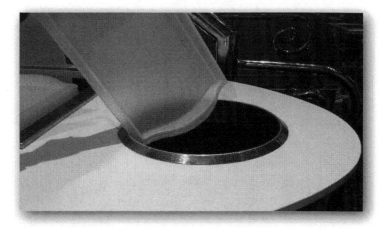

It didn't! This garbage receptacle had been carefully designed with the user experience of two different constituents in mind:

1) The customer, in order to make it as easy as possible to get rid of trash; and
2) The pastry shop, in order to prevent the added expense of trays being accidentally thrown away

Compare that to the last hot dog restaurant you went to, which likely had a sign near the garbage can: "Please don't throw away the baskets." This was a genius solution, and it struck me that somebody actually gave some thought to the design of a garbage receptacle – something that most customers would never notice.

Now if that garbage can wowed me (you might think I'm easy to impress), the sleek new bathroom sink faucets at a popular hotel chain that I frequent did not. I noticed the faucets immediately because, well, I notice these kinds of things now, and because I had stayed at this hotel enough times to recognize that they had been changed. It was a nice-looking faucet, but the problem was that when I went to fill the iron, I couldn't get any water into it because it didn't fit underneath the new faucet!

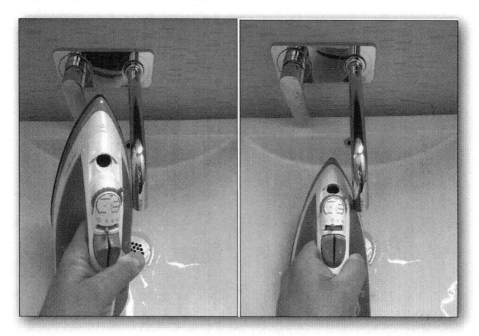

Frustrated but undeterred because my shirts were pretty wrinkled, I created a manual system whereby I cupped water in my hand and carefully fed the little hole on the top of the iron. It took a long time, and it was then that I realized that in this case, no one thought through the entire user experience of the new faucet. My guess is that the person in charge of faucets and the person in charge of irons are two different people, and they did not collaborate on this project.

User experience examples are everywhere. Have you ever tried to plug in your electronic device on a plane that has the plugs between the seats right near the floor?

You have to essentially put your head in your lap, turn the flashlight on your phone to even see the plug, and fish around until you can plug in the cord the right way – all with your head close to some stranger's feet. Newer planes have moved the plugs to just inside the tray tables, which is a much easier user experience.

You may have heard of a company called Uber that is taking over the taxi industry. If you've ever used Uber, you know that the startup identified practically every consumer pain point involved with hailing a taxi – not being able to find one, standing in a long taxi line, rude drivers, the credit card machine always being broken – and addressed each one with a simple, brilliant mobile app.

What you might not know is something I learned from talking with a friendly Uber driver in Seattle – that the company also identified and addressed practically every *driver* pain point, too. My Seattle Uber driver told me that at a traditional taxi company, she had to pay a fortune for a taxi medallion, and even with that monthly payment she was not covered by auto insurance, which Uber provides without requiring a medallion. She had to carry a lot of cash and was constantly afraid of being robbed. She had to work specified hours instead of determining her own schedule.

Hopefully you get the point – Uber is such a classic example because it figured out how to create a simple, clean experience for both the customer and the driver. When both sides work in perfect harmony, everyone enjoys the experience. The taxi industry didn't see Uber coming, and has been slow to innovate in response.

Remember that the little things matter. Every single interaction with your company is an opportunity to create an advocate or alienate a customer.

Now what do all these customer experience and user experience examples have to do with social media? Read on to find out.

SOCIAL MEDIA'S ROLE IN CUSTOMER EXPERIENCE

I f you don't get the offline experience right, you will suffer the consequences in social media.

These days, everyone with a smartphone can snap a photo of their poor experience and post it to Facebook or Twitter in mere moments – and they're doing so, at an alarming rate. When this happens, their friends or followers are now witnesses to the experience and often engage in discussion and share with their friends or followers as well.

Social media has fundamentally changed how people communicate with each other. Customer Service Consultant and Author John R. DiJulius III calls social media the "biggest influence on Customer Service in 50 years" in his book, *The Customer Service Revolution*. In fact, he said, "Social media has turned Customer Service upside down."[1]

Social media has also given consumers the power to amplify their customer experience – positive or negative – by sharing it with friends, fans, and followers. This is why it is so essential for companies to get the offline experience right.

"If you don't remember what the customer wants, they're only a click away from ranting about it, tweeting about it publicly or phoning you and increasing your expense," said Joshua March, CEO of Social Customer Care platform Conversocial. "So it's really got to be done well."[2]

When experiences get shared, it is incumbent upon the brand to respond and engage.

"Social media has changed things," said Shep Hyken. "Customers have a bigger voice than ever before and therefore I believe it raises the bar for every company to do an effective job."[3]

Companies that already have a culture of Customer Service are able to face this challenge head-on without fear. According *The Definitive Guide to Social, Mobile Customer Service (Volume 4)* by Conversocial, "Unless your social media Customer Service strategy is powered by an underlying drive to provide exceptional customer experience, you aren't built on the right foundation for social customer maturity."[4]

"We look at social media as purely an extension to the digitization of all aspects of our lives," said Monty Hamilton, head of digital operations at Telstra, Australia's leading telecommunications company. "Conversations that used to take place physically are taking place in digital environments... We need to simply be ready for our customers' change in appetite to deal with us in different channels."[5]

A brand's decision to engage or ignore contributes a great deal to the customer's overall perception of the brand.

Did the brand respond to my post?
NO → Why not? Am I not important enough of a customer? Am I not influential enough in social media?
YES → How long did the response take? Did the company demonstrate an appropriate level of empathy? Did they solve my problem if I had one?

These are all questions which will color the overall customer experience.

"People understand that we're there, we're quickly responding and we're really good at the experience part as well," explained Michelle Mattson, Director of Social Media at T-Mobile. "So we've got a lot of repeat customers." This is critical because T-Mobile is changing customers' minds about Customer Service in social media – those that begin using the channel as a last resort often end up coming back to it as a first resort.[6]

Scotty's Brewhouse reads and responds to every social media post, in some cases affecting the service in the restaurant in real-time. Wise believes that his restaurants' ability to provide real-time service – whether it's at the physical locations or online – can affect a customer's experience even more than the food.

"I tell my managers that I'd love to get no tweets and no emails because that tells me that my management team is on the floor taking care of guests, whether they're having a good experience or a negative experience," said Wise. "If they get to that table and take care of that negative experience right away, they can do the same thing I'm doing in person vs. me doing it on Twitter, [and] then they've accomplished exactly what I'm asking them to do."[7]

Incidentally, Twitter has done some incredible research which looked at the benefits to companies, beyond an improved customer experience, of responding quickly to inquiries on the platform. They found that a customer's willingness to spend more with the company, and the overall satisfaction scores, were both higher when companies responded on Twitter. In addition, faster responses equated to even higher spending. We will review the Twitter research in more detail in Chapter 4.

WHAT GETS SHARED?

After interviewing dozens of brands for the *Focus on Customer Service* podcast and analyzing a plethora of posts directed at brands, I have developed a very simple formula for determining what gets shared. It is:

EXPECTATIONS + EMOTIONS = WILLINGNESS TO SHARE

All of your customers have expectations about what their experience should be like with your brand. The vast majority of those expectations are perfectly reasonable – I want it to be fast, easy, friendly, reasonably priced, and so on. How your brand performs against those expectations has a strong influence on whether your customers will share their experience on social media.

- If a brand EXCEEDS expectations, customers are HAPPY, and their willingness to share their experience in social media is HIGH.
- If a brand simply MEETS expectations, customers are neither happy nor sad ("MEH," as some might say), and the willingness to share their experience is LOW.
- If a brand MISSES expectations, customers are UNHAPPY (or even ANGRY), and unfortunately their willingness to share their experience is VERY HIGH.

Most experiences fall into the MEETS category and therefore are not shared on social media. That presents an enormous opportunity for brands to be able to control some of the social media conversation – by ensuring that brand experiences consistently fall into the EXCEEDS category. A smart strategy in social is to make sure that your positive experiences are amplified and that you are able to reduce or at least learn from negative experiences. Missed expectations – and the resulting negative posts – allow a brand to learn about what is not working with its product or service, and provide an opportunity to demonstrate outstanding Customer Service in a public setting.

"We're so apt as a society to tell people when they do wrong or what they did bad," said Wise of Scotty's Brewhouse. "I've always told my customers: come to me first. If you tell me that I'm doing something wrong and I still don't fix it, then you have every right to blast me and never come back again. But at least give me the opportunity."[8]

The more polarized the elicited emotion, the more likely the customer is to share his or her experience online. That's why we often see both really positive and really negative product reviews or social media posts. Very few people ever go online to share that the experience they had was just OK.

So what can brands do? The answer is to focus as much on the offline experience as the online experience, since the former may quickly become the latter.

OFFLINE CAN COME ONLINE AT ANY TIME

In today's day and age, when the emotion is "frustration" at not being able to iron your shirt in a hotel room, what do you think is going to happen? The hotel chain is likely going to see a public complaint on social media. These are avoidable, but companies have to be aware of the user experience and consider multiple use cases. In the case of the hotel faucet, one has to consider the many ways someone might use a sink: washing hands, brushing teeth, shaving, ironing, filling a water bottle, making coffee, and cleaning clothes.

One other thing to keep in mind: Your social media marketing will draw out Customer Service inquiries, often about topics that are not even related to your marketing message. As much as we don't want to admit it, most of the time our customers aren't thinking about our brand. We are thinking about it all the time, but our customers have other things on their mind. They are going about their daily lives, worrying about work and the kids and what they are going to make for dinner that night. Our brand becomes relevant to them when they are ready for it – unless we interrupt their day with marketing.

While that marketing may do a terrific job of increasing brand awareness, or getting people to perform some desired call to action, it also reminds people about their experience with our brand. And when we have missed expectations with that experience, our marketing message serves as a reminder that the customer was wanting to complain to us about something. Ironically, our social media marketing message has given them the very public chance of doing so.

WHAT YOU NEED TO DO

Now that we have identified what encompasses customer experience and user experience, it is time to start thinking about what companies need to do to succeed. There is a lot of complexity here, so don't feel like you have to achieve perfection immediately. As Mattson noted: "I like to say we're building the plane as we're flying it" – and T-Mobile is already one of the best in the business at social Customer Service. "I think we have good handle on it," she added, "but the fun part for me is there's always something new, there's always new challenge."[9]

To answer the question of what you need to do to ensure a great customer experience, I turn to the great sage Joe Maddon, manager of the World Champion Chicago Cubs. Among Joe's many "Maddonisms" (which apply both to baseball and business) is this gem: "Do Simple Better." In baseball, Maddon is talking about always making the routine plays, whether it's fielding a ground ball, sliding into second, or laying down a bunt. In business, this equates to making every interaction with the customer easier.[10]

Simplicity is a basic tenet of customer experience, but it is often overlooked in favor of a company's outdated rules or procedures. Doing simple better means aiming for the fewest clicks (or taps) possible to complete a digital task, allowing a customer to easily talk to a human being on the phone if they need to, and writing legal terms and conditions in language customers can understand.

Some companies have embraced simplicity since their inception. Take Google, for example. Is there anything simpler than Google's home page, with just a search bar and two buttons? (I have never understood why they have kept the "I Feel Lucky" button all this time, but that is irrelevant here.) Compare Google's home page to Yahoo's home page, and it might start to explain the different trajectories of their stock prices. Google is the essence of simplicity.

Some companies are marred by excessive government regulation, making simplicity nearly impossible. I have worked in two such industries – financial services and healthcare – and have determined that while the government usually has noble intentions, its overly prescriptive remedies often miss the mark, sometimes creating the opposite of the desired effect.

For example, a certain government agency wants to ensure that consumers understand the contract they are signing with a company. As a steward of great customer experiences, I completely agree with that goal. If we assume a level of honesty and integrity on the part of the companies, we can assume that they don't want a consumer signing up for something they don't understand any more than the government does. But a typical government solution is to require a ridiculously lengthy legal disclosure. Sure, that might provide every detail that any consumer could ever imagine, but does it really solve the problem of making things more understandable for the customer?

DO SIMPLE BETTER. Think about every touch point your company has with its prospects and customers, and ask yourself if you are talking in their language, or yours. Ask yourself if you can turn two clicks into a single click (My bank makes me select the account where I want to deposit a check on the mobile app every single time, even though I only have one account!). Ask yourself if the "routine" elements of the experience – like a routine grounder to the shortstop in baseball – are actually routine, or anything but?

Doing simple better also means getting the basics right in your business. It means minimizing errors or unnecessary delays, sending out communications that have correct spelling and grammar, keeping the physical space in which customers are present clean and tidy at all times, and answering the telephone when a customer calls.

One of my favorite examples of doing simple better occurred when I was waiting for a conference call to begin. Usually, there is horrible hold music that, if you use the same conferencing system over and over like at work, gets stuck in your head. (More than once I have caught myself walking down a hallway humming the conference call hold song!) On this occasion, however, I immediately noticed that the music was different. There was a guitar strumming and then a guy singing who was actually good. And what's that? The lyrics to the song were about waiting on hold for a conference call – and they were hilarious!

Well I've been sitting here all day, I've been sitting in this waiting room
And I've been waiting on my friends, yes I'm waiting on this conference
call – all alone
And I'm on hold – yes, I'm on hold – I hope it's not all day!
Well I wonder where they are, yes I wonder where my friends have gone
(Where'd they go?)
Tell me, where could they be while I'm waiting on this conference call? (I
don't know.)

Well I'm holding on the phone, yes I'm holding on the line
I don't know where they are, I don't know why I'm still alone.

(The song is called "I'm On Hold" by singer Alex Cornell. I encourage you to listen to the rest of it on YouTube![11])

See what he did there? He took something simple – waiting on hold – and made it better. So much better, in fact, that I found myself hoping the other party would wait to join the call until the song was over! This is a great example of turning a mundane experience into a completely memorable one.

Here's another example of doing simple better. You know that legal nonsense that you sometimes see at the end of emails sent from corporations? The reminder that if you are not the intended recipient of this communication, that you are obliged to delete it and not hold the company responsible for sending it to you in the first place?

Most of us ignore this disclosure because it's filled with legalese that we don't understand. But would you ignore a disclosure that started with, in all caps, COVERING OUR BUTTS? Malaysian video-on-demand service iflix uses this at the end of its corporate emails:

COVERING OUR BUTTS: We know this email message and any accompanying attachments are full of fun and intriguing stuff, but they may contain information that is confidential and is subject to legal privilege. In other words, we could tell you, but then we'd have to kill you. Just kidding. There are other ways: If you are not the intended recipient, do not read, use, disseminate (it means "spread"), distribute or copy this message or attachments. If you have received this message in error (oops, our bad), please notify the sender immediately and delete the message. Any views, or bad jokes, expressed in this message, are those of the individual sender, except where the individual sender expressly states them to be the views of iflix (even the bad jokes). Before opening any attachments, please check them for viruses, defects and prepare to be amazed by the iflix revolution.[12]

Did you read every word like I did? Can you believe it held your attention as long as it did, given that it wasn't marketing or advertising? The reason is that this company did simple better, in a surprising way that improved an otherwise mundane experience.

What does it look like when a company does not "do simple better"? Let's look at a chat session between a friend of mine and a Canadian telecom company.

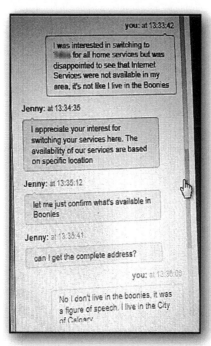

My friend had a simple request; in fact, he was looking to become this company's newest customer. "I was interested in switching to [Company] for all home services but was disappointed to see that Internet Services were not available in my area. It's not like I live in the Boonies," he wrote. The Customer Service agent's answer? "Let me just confirm what's available in Boonies. Can I get the complete address?" Yikes. Sure, it's a simple mistake. But doing simple better makes all the difference in the world when it comes to customer experience.

By the way, can you guess how I found this screenshot? It was posted on Facebook!

CREATING A "WOW" MOMENT

Eric Tung is a social media influencer who I had the pleasure of meeting at Social Media Marketing World, the country's largest social media conference held annually in San Diego. Eric decided to find out if hotels actually read that field in the booking process which asks for "special requests." Clearly in a playful mood, Eric asked the Grand Hyatt San Diego for a picture of a pickle and some chocolate. Since he booked his hotel weeks before the conference, he promptly forgot about his request. Imagine his surprise when he arrived at his room: There was a drawing of a pickle – complete with crayons to color it in – and a Snickers bar! Eric immediately tweeted:

The letter from the hotel reads: "Welcome! When we were looking over your reservation we noticed that you were requesting a picture of a pickle and a piece of chocolate to enjoy. Here at the Manchester Grand Hyatt San Diego we want to make sure your needs aren't just met they are exceeded. Have fun coloring in this pickle and enjoy your time at the Social Media Marketing World Conference 2015! Let us know if you need anything else."

As it turns out, Eric Tung isn't just any guy on social media; at the time of this tweet, he had more than 146,000 followers on Twitter. His tweet, which also included the conference hashtag (and a conference hashtag at a social media conference usually ends up trending on Twitter), was retweeted more than 200 times and favorited almost 300 times!

The average Twitter user has 208 followers, according to multiple sources on the internet, which sounds about right. But since Eric is a well-known social media influencer, many of his followers are undoubtedly other influencers who have far more followers. Let's conservatively estimate that the average of Eric's follower's followers is 500 (remember, he has 146,000!). With 209 retweets, his complimentary tweet had the potential to reach more than 100,000 people *in addition to his own followers*. All because the Grand Hyatt San Diego actually read the "special requests" box and acted on it. That's doing simple better.

Scott Wise of Scotty's Brewhouse knows there are thousands of other restaurants out there. "So what makes us any different than any one of them? There's only one thing: and that's the human being that is serving them the food, that is entertaining them, that is getting them the check when they want to get out or that is going above and beyond," he said. "It's not just serving the food – that's expected. I tell them to go above and beyond... to give somebody something they want that they never knew they wanted. That's when you create a 'wow' moment."[13]

3

WHY SOCIAL CUSTOMER CARE

Before we begin talking about the "how" of Social Customer Care, it's important to take some time to think about the "why." Deciding to offer Customer Service in social media just because everyone else is doing it will certainly not set you up to succeed. You and your team need a foundational set of beliefs that will drive how you execute your Social Customer Care program. You also need an organization that is committed to Customer Service.

Companies that are already good at Customer Service have a huge advantage in social media because it then becomes just another channel to do what they are already doing well, which is listening to customers, responding and engaging. For companies where Customer Service has not been a priority in the past, social media becomes a much more difficult place to be because expectations are enormously high. You can't hide behind a telephone and a long hold time anymore.

Take a moment to think about why you're interested in providing Customer Service in social media. What are the benefits? What are the risks? Consider that executives at your company may think you're certifiably crazy just for broaching the topic. But you know better; for example, you know that one of the main reasons to offer Social Customer Care is because your customers are demanding it. They're already on Facebook, Twitter, and other platforms talking about your brand and asking questions. You might as well be part of that conversation, right? Otherwise someone else – including a competitor – might swoop in and handle those conversations for you.

Convincing management that your customers are demanding Social Customer Care shouldn't be difficult, but make sure you have some data to validate this assertion. Simple listening tools or even Twitter's and Facebook's native search functionality should provide you with more than enough information about what is being said about your brand, how often your brand is mentioned, and what the general tone is. Grab a few screenshots of the particularly memorable brand mentions to show your bosses, and make sure to include both positive and negative mentions.

Keep in mind that the volume of Customer Service mentions in social media will likely be far less than the telephone or email or chat, so it may be hard to get an operation center's attention. But call centers inherently understand why Social Customer Care is important because they understand that it's important to respond to customers. It will be up to you to help them incorporate Social Customer Care into their existing ecosystem, while maintaining the somewhat unique approach that is necessary in this unique channel.

"Social media is increasingly not only a foundational channel your customer turns to for help, but slowly overtaking the pillars of what have been considered the mainstays of modern Customer Service," notes Conversocial in its *Definitive Guide*. "Customers' expectations have changed, as have their patience, options and communication styles. Archaic phone, IVR, email and chat functionality will not cut it anymore." The *Definitive Guide* adds: "Social Customer Service is not merely an added channel to the service ecosystem, but rather the catalyst that's redefining how legacy channels interact with their audience."[1]

Other reasons to offer Social Customer Care may include:

- Acquiring customer feedback on your products and services in order to constantly iterate and improve your offerings
- Helping to solve customer problems that were not solved in other Customer Service channels
- Being present for Millennials and others who are learning that obtaining Customer Service in social media is much easier and quicker than in other channels
- Reducing cost in your Customer Service department, since social Customer Service is usually less expensive to administer than telephone service

- Improving your brand perception by appearing to be friendly, empathetic, and helpful

"Try to minimize the amount of people calling in," suggests Sparkcentral's white paper, *7 Steps To Kickstart A Social Customer Service Strategy*. "Give them another savvier, swifter avenue to pursue you, i.e. social media. We all know calls are the most expensive way to communicate with customers, with the exception of flying into town to meet with them face to face and shaking their hands. Any way you are able to divert those calls are not only going to save you money and make your daily operations more profitable... but it will make your customers happy."[2]

RESPONDING ON SOCIAL MEDIA

This book will provide a plethora of tips and best practices for responding to Customer Service inquiries on social media. But first, it is instructive to think about why social media is different from other Customer Service channels such as telephone, email, click-to-chat, and in-person service.

Social media is:

- **Public.** It is, in fact, the world's only public Customer Service channel.
- **Searchable.** Anyone can search for your brand along with other keywords on Facebook, Twitter, Google, and other sites.
- **Shareable.** Any post on a social media site – whether from a customer or a brand – is instantly shareable by any user.
- **Permanent.** Social media is pretty much forever. Sure, there are exceptions – one's own posts can be deleted on most sites and brands can "hide" posts from others on their Facebook page – but the majority of posts stay on the site forever.

The social media ecosystem requires that brands talk *with* consumers instead of *at* them. This is often a new concept for traditional brand marketers, who are used to being able to completely control the brand message with TV and print advertising that is akin to shouting with a megaphone. The problem with this approach is that no one wakes up in the morning and checks Facebook or Twitter or Instagram hoping to hear from a brand. But people are indeed interested in engaging with brands they like, and social media is a great channel for that. You may have to occasionally remind your Marketing friends not to forget the "social" in social media.

"I think the beauty of the internet and social media is what it's done to our world by kind of compressing it and making it much smaller," said Scott Wise of Scotty's Brewhouse. "It's not just a one-way conversation, that's not how it should work."[3]

Consumers have a choice – and a voice – on social media; they don't have to listen to brands, and they are free to "talk back," making it a two-way conversation. This shifts the power from the brand to the consumer. And since consumers are tired of substandard Customer Service in traditional channels, they have capitalized on the opportunity to share their experiences in public.

"I think what the most important thing to realize for brands today is that customers have been going to these channels like Twitter and Facebook to circumvent your internal processes," said Sparkcentral CEO Davy Kestens. "The entire enterprise Customer Service model has been broken for the last few decades."[4]

Customer Service on social media can also be critiqued more publicly than other channels. When brands surprise and delight their customers, positive brand mentions skyrocket. But on the flipside, we have all heard of classic screw-ups by brands on social media, which also causes stories to "go viral."

What's more, your customers and prospective customers are comparing you against every other brand out there – not just your direct competitors.

"What's happened is when I have a great experience on Delta Airlines and then I go to any other business I say, 'Why can't they be as friendly as the people that took care of me on Delta Airlines?'" said Customer Service expert Shep Hyken. "If I go to a restaurant and I'm treated well and then I go to a bookstore, I'm going to compare the person who's apathetic, introverted, not outgoing, barely talks to me, barely looks at me, to the friendly server that I had the night before. And if I'm doing B2B business and I'm talking with an inside service rep [who] is really helpful, and then I call another company and

I don't get that same type of help – and they're not even competing businesses, not even in the same industry – I'm comparing them."[5]

As a rule, I don't like to call out brands for their public failures. The negative PR is bad enough that they don't need people like me piling on. But one example I like to share demonstrates why the stakes are so high, and what can happen even when a brand gets it right.

In February of 2016, conservative commentator Amanda Carpenter tweeted at Amtrak: "Guys. I'm trapped in an Amtrak elevator at BWI airport. Help?"[6] Amtrak responded, "We are sorry to hear that. Are you still in the elevator?"[7] Seems like an appropriate response, until one notices that the answer came *7 months later*! The internet went crazy. It was a lead story on Mashable ("Amtrak asks woman if she's still trapped in elevator months later"[8]); it got its own segment on *The Today Show* ("Amtrak responds to a woman stuck in elevator… seven months later"[9]); and there were tons of viral "memes" showing Amanda's profile picture devolved into a skeleton.

So what went wrong? For that we need to start with a little detective work – something that much of the media skipped. It turns out that Amtrak actually did respond to Amanda (albeit still 2 hours and 16 minutes after Amanda's tweet) with this message: "BWI agents are aware of you, and are working to get you out."[10] Of course, Amanda's story had a happy ending, as she was indeed rescued from the elevator that same day.

Amtrak both responded and resolved Amanda's issue, but still ended up getting skewered in the media and on social media. The culprit? A new Customer Service agent at Amtrak who saw Amanda's original tweet retweeted seven months later and thought it was a new tweet. This was a simple, yet costly mistake because of the public nature of this particular Customer Service channel. But it serves as a good reminder that even the companies doing Social Customer Care well are susceptible to public scrutiny, so it pays to have an efficient, optimized system with proper controls in place to prevent mistakes.

Or as David Tull, customer engagement manager of Jack Threads, puts it: "Yes, social media Customer Service is in public so the stakes are higher. Rather than see that as a liability, see that as an opportunity."[11]

SOCIAL CUSTOMER CARE BY THE NUMBERS

According to research done by author and speaker Jay Baer for his book, *Hug Your Haters*, with the help of Edison Research, 62% of first complaints are made by phone or email.[12] That statistic tells us that many social media complaints are from customers who are turning to the public channel as a last resort – because other Customer Service channels failed them.

Have you ever waited on hold forever, or not been able to navigate through a long menu of options to get to a human being? Have you ever sent a company an email but never received a human response? Has the live chat function ever been "Unavailable" on a website just when you needed it? When this happens, people turn to social media. And not surprisingly, these customers are unhappy or angry to start because the brand has already missed expectations.

Even more worrisome is that only 40% of social media complaints are addressed by brands.[13] This statistic continues to confound me because social media is no longer a shiny new channel; it has been around for more than a decade at this point, and Customer Service has been present on it from the beginning. When other service channels fail and then a customer is ignored on social media, one has to assume that their relationship with the brand is about to come to an end.

"When someone tweets at your brand, the worst response is no response," writes Bryan Kramer in his book, *There is no B2B or B2C: It's Human to Human: #H2H.*[14] Or as Dave Kerpen, CEO of Likeable Media said, "Not responding is a response. A response that says 'I don't care about you.'"[15] Yet this is still happening 60% of the time in social media! Your business can – and needs to be – different.

Baer's research also found that among customers who expect a response in social media, nearly 40% expect that response within one hour, but that the average response time of brands that bother to respond at all is just under five hours.[16] Is that meeting or exceeding expectations? I think not. This statistic reminds me of an unattributed Customer Service joke, "If I had wanted my question answered two hours from now, I would have waited two hours to ask my question."

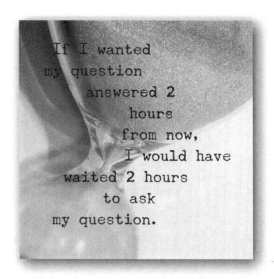

If I wanted
my question
answered 2
hours
from now,
I would have
waited 2 hours
to ask
my question.

Finally, Baer's research determined that responding to a complaint on social media increases customer advocacy by 25%, and not responding decreases customer advocacy by 45%.[17] Multiply that by the number of complaints that an average Fortune 500 company receives on social media – no matter what business they're in – and this can equate to millions of dollars of lost sales.

This is why I often say that "Customer Service is the New Marketing." Brands spend millions of dollars – sometimes tens or even hundreds of millions – every year in marketing and advertising, with the main goal often being brand awareness and consideration. But those same brands are willing to let their own customers go unanswered on social media, resulting in *lost* brand consideration. It makes no sense. The best explanation I can come up with is that most large companies still operate in silos – so the Marketing budget and the Customer Service budget are in two different places, with two different sets of goals. The more that companies realize that these two critical departments are inextricably linked, the more they will be able to optimize their investment dollar.

Let's look at a couple of examples of how valuable a good Customer Service response in social media can be. Discover Card received a tweet that said, "Haven't checked my mail in a few days and there are 3 offers for the @Discover it card. Persistence or lack of coordination?"[18] I absolutely loved the agent's response, which demonstrated the perfect amount of humor while remaining professional and addressing the issue:

"We must be excited to have you apply! DM w/ your full name & full address if you would like the mailings to stop. *Amy"[19]

What's great about this response?

1) It contained just the right amount of snarkiness (mirroring his tone)
2) It still managed to help him solve his problem
3) Amy personalized the experience by signing her name at the end

You might be surprised at what the person tweeted next.

"@Discover kudos for the prompt response time! Ok I'll bite, mostly because of your response Amy. #greatservice"[20]

You read that right. A person who started off as a Discover detractor ended up applying for a Discover Card! Why? Because Discover exceeded his expectations. He might have just been venting; he probably thought Discover would ignore him like so many other brands do. Instead, he received a humorous, personalized response just nine minutes after his initial tweet. And in just 13 minutes, Discover found a brand-new customer and advocate.

That illustrates the power of Customer Service in social media. This simply doesn't happen in other Customer Service channels.

Here is another example that was shared with me on an episode of the *Focus on Customer Service* podcast by Chug Abramson, Vice President of Global Customer Service and Social Media, and Sam Thomas, Global Manager of Social Media Support for the music streaming company Spotify[21]:

Steve, a Spotify customer, sent a snarky tweet telling the company "you guys had one job" and included a screenshot of some legal language that contained the word "authorise." (The customer was teasing Spotify for spelling the word with the British "s" instead of the American "z.")

Spotify's response was brilliant:

"Hi Steve! Thanks for bringing this to us. Maybe we can explain why this happened…" The response also included a link, which sent Steve to this Spotify playlist:

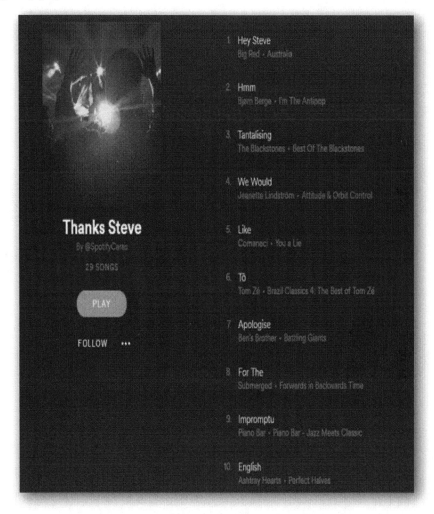

Look carefully. Read the titles of the songs from top to bottom, and you will see that Spotify has embedded its answer into the playlist! (The full list of song titles reads: "Hey Steve/Hmm/Tantalising/We Would/Like/Tô/Apologise/For

The/Impromptu/English/UK/Lesson/We Were/Just/Trying To/Bring/A Little/ Colour/To/Your Day/Shout/If/There's/Anything Else/I'm off/To/Catch/An/ Aeroplane" – and yes, they are all real songs!)

This is a really innovative (and awesome) use of their own product to deliver memorable Customer Service. Steve loved it, tweeting back: "This is amazing, thank you Spotify" – with a heart emoji, of course.

Whether it's Discover mirroring a poster's tone to perfection, or Spotify leveraging its own product in a creative fashion, examples abound of companies creating memorable experiences in social media with outstanding Customer Service.

So why is this the new marketing? Because the value that companies can get in terms of brand awareness, brand consideration, and brand loyalty from outstanding public Customer Service can far outweigh what is gained from great marketing. As we will discuss in Chapter 9: Reporting, some companies have seen a 100% or more engagement rate on Customer Service posts *after* the issue was resolved. That means that satisfied customers are still liking, sharing, and retweeting even after the transaction has finished. Ask any marketer what their best engagement rate is, and you will hear many citing single digit percentages, with some really good ones citing double digits into the 30s. But 100% or more is unheard of.

THE "WOW" MOMENT REVISITED

Remember Eric Tung, the guy who asked for a picture of a pickle and a chocolate bar while staying at the Grand Hyatt San Diego? His story didn't end there. As we discussed above, Customer Service is one of the key components of customer experience, and the offline and online portions of an experience often overlap. Nowhere is this more evident than with the end of Eric's story.

After his trip to San Diego, Eric was traveling to Amelia Island, Florida and staying at a Residence Inn – which is a completely different hotel chain. Imagine Eric's surprise when he entered that hotel room – and found this:

This time, the picture is of the Rugrats family (the baby is called Pickles) and it is accompanied by a fancy bar of chocolate (and a dining and spa voucher!). The note reads: "Mr. Tung – Heard you like pickles and chocolate – am I doing this right? Thanks for staying with us…"

The Residence Inn Amelia actually took an online experience – they clearly witnessed Eric's public Twitter interaction with the Grand Hyatt San Diego – and brought it back offline, but delivering Eric's pickle and chocolate request in a different way *without him even having to ask for it*. This is an incredible example of social listening, knowing your customer, having the permission to surprise and delight a customer, and integrating public knowledge with your CRM (Customer Relationship Management) system. CRM will be discussed more in Chapter 11.

WHAT DO I NEED TO DO?

I am glad you asked that question, because that is what this book is really about. Now that you understand the basics of Customer Experience, and the interplay between offline and online experience, you can start the journey of building an outstanding Customer Service operation in social media. As I like to say: "Customer Experience is Everything – because it can all end up on social media!"

You will need to start with a Philosophy, which we will discuss in Chapter 4. That Philosophy can be tailored to your company, but to be most successful, it must include the goal of "Respond to Everyone."

Let's briefly go back to our three different kinds of customer emotions based on experience, and look at how we should respond to each of them:

EXCEEDS (HAPPY): Say thank you, engage, and show some love back
MEETS (MEH): Answer the question, engage, and educate
MISSES (UNHAPPY, ANGRY): Empathize, engage, and try to solve the problem

Notice a theme? In each case, the word "engage" is part of the response. This is critical given that so many brands are still ignoring social media posts from customers, yet customers have high expectations for a quick brand response. So in essence, brands have a new opportunity to exceed, meet, or miss customers' expectations of a particular experience – and this time, it is in public for everyone to see. Is this the time to run and hide? NO! By engaging everyone who takes time out of their day to interact with your brand, you will make far more friends than enemies (or in social media speak, far more advocates than detractors).

THE "8 STEPS TO WINNING AT SOCIAL CUSTOMER CARE"

After you have established your Philosophy (Step #1), you will need to address the other Winning at Social Customer Care Steps – selecting the appropriate Technology (#2), selecting a Team (#3), Training that team (#4), establishing a repeatable Process (#5), and creating management Reporting (#6). Then, if you are really advanced, you can look at Integrating with the Core Business (#7) and Integrating with CRM (#8).

Let's start with the first step.

4

PHILOSOPHY
(WINNING AT SOCIAL CUSTOMER CARE STEP #1)

Your Philosophy should be borne out of your company's Vision, Mission, and/or Values, preferably with some piece of it originating from the top of the organization. This ensures employee buy-in at every level.

Scott Wise of Scotty's Brewhouse said he learned from his father, also a businessman, that treating people the right way (embodying your company's Values) must start from the top:

"I remember my dad pulling into his office, and he parked like four miles away from the front door and I said, 'Dad, you own the company, why aren't you parking right by the door?' And he said, 'Because Scott, you never forget that you're no better than any single person in this company or this world. You are all equal. And just because you're name's on the building or because you sign the paychecks... you will gain more respect out of the people that are working with you and you'll find that they will move mountains for you by doing little things like this and showing them that you are their equal, and you're working right there in the trenches with them.'"

Wise continued: "And so I just have always run my company with this open door policy... I tell people any time they need something personally or professionally, I want them to come in and talk to me because I'll always give them an open and honest answer, and I think by doing that and showing people that respect and giving them the same thing that you would want in return, you're going to get so much out of your people and out of your business."[1]

Your Social Customer Care Philosophy should include the guiding principles that will enable your execution strategy. These are the "guardrails" that you establish to define your offering, and should be specific to your customers' (and company's) needs.

Things to consider include:

Brand Voice: What do you want your brand to stand for in social media? Is your brand funny and irreverent or serious and fact-driven?

"We've been working with our Communications and Marketing team to develop what is our online voice. We have a very diverse team. Everybody has their own individual voice," said Rob Hahn, assistant manager of Social Customer Care at Southwest Airlines. "So we're taking items from our new branding…and determining what do we want our online voice to be to match our brand and to match our Philosophy of providing excellent Customer Service."[2]

Incidentally, the corporate mission of Southwest Airlines, as stated on its website, is "dedication to the highest quality of Customer Service delivered with a sense of warmth, friendliness, individual pride, and Company Spirit."[3]

Authenticity is a key component of brand voice, said Telstra's Monty Hamilton. "Just because you're having an interaction in a new and different channel doesn't mean you need to change who you are," he said.[4]

Scott Wise added: "I think what the guests and the consumer enjoys is that the brand is an actual person."[5]

Availability: Should you offer Social Customer Care 24 hours a day, 7 days a week? It depends. In some industries, like multi-national airlines and hotels, customers have questions or problems around the clock so it's critical that service is available. Do you have international customers, or customers who travel frequently and may need to contact you from abroad? Is your product or service available 24/7? For example, a local pizza restaurant that is only open for lunch and dinner need not worry about 24/7 Social Customer Care. But a credit card, hospital, or convenience store may be available all day and all night, which increases the likelihood of customers needing help at odd hours.

"We believe that we need to be available when our customers want to interact with us as opposed to indoctrinating certain service hours to our customers," said Telstra's Monty Hamilton. "Australians love to travel and they take their products and services on the road with them. So if I land at Charles de Gaulle Airport in Paris and my global roaming is not turned on on my phone, it's not really important to me what time it is in Australia. I need my telephone to be working and to connect back with home…It might be 3 a.m. in Australia and perfect broad daylight in Paris. We need to be available to support customers."[6]

Availability isn't just binary, however. If you are not going to offer 24/7 service it's still important to determine the hours of operation. Just because your company's headquarters is on the East Coast of the United States doesn't mean there aren't customers on the West Coast – three time zones away – who may need help during their business hours. So consider the needs of your customers when determining your company's availability. And if possible, try to mimic the hours of your other Customer Service channels.

"We don't all work 9 to 5 anymore… we're working different hours and we're consuming content and personal life experiences during the day that we used to reserve to during the night," Hamilton said. "So our lives have changed. And therefore when we choose to interact with organizations has also changed with that."[7] In other words, let your customers dictate your working hours, not the other way around.

If your service is not 24/7, you should be sure to clearly indicate your hours of availability on your page. Twitter allows you to choose the time periods in which you are "most responsive," and Facebook allows you to indicate when you are "Away" and not answering inquiries. Both platforms allow you to send automated direct message responses if desired. (Facebook distinguishes between "Away Messages" and "Instant Replies," the latter of which is sent automatically to people who message for the first time[8]. Twitter's nomenclature for "Instant Replies" is "Welcome Messages."[9])

You should also consider sending proactive "Good morning" and "Good night" tweets to alert customers that your service agents are on duty or are going home for the night. (This is not practical on Facebook.) Before Discover went to 24/7 service in social media, the company used a creative agency to develop "opening and closing" tweets with fun, memorable messages that actually resulted in high levels of engagement on their own.

Languages: Similar to Availability, the languages you decide to support in Customer Service should depend on customers' needs. Two rules of thumb that would suggest multilingual support is necessary are whether you are marketing your product or service in another language, and whether other Customer Service channels offer additional language support.

Social Media Platforms: Deciding the social media platforms in which you will offer Customer Service can be tricky, but again, focus on your customer. "Is this person a customer? Yes. Do we care about our customers? Yes. Well, we should support them," said Sparkcentral's Davy Kestens.[10]

Dan Moriarty, formerly of Hyatt Hotels and now the director of digital for the Chicago Bulls, agrees. "I always hated that question of 'how many of our customers are there?' because I think as soon as the answer is one, if they're willing to talk to you or wanting to talk to you, technology should be scaled in a way that makes it a marginal incremental cost for a business," he said on one of our podcast episodes.[11]

Most brands in the U.S. start with Twitter, since the vast majority of Customer Service inquiries in social media occur there and the platform itself promotes the service use case.

"Twitter have come out and said, 'We view Customer Service as a real strategic priority for us' and they're investing very heavily on a lot of very specific service functionality," said Conversocial's Joshua March. "The fact is in the U.S., social Customer Service in general really means Twitter. And Twitter is kind of synonymous with Customer Service. Any brand that is serious about social service in any way is going be heavily on Twitter."[12]

Next up is Facebook, which virtually every brand is already on for marketing purposes because it is by far the largest social media platform, but it often places second in the U.S. in terms of Customer Service volume (although many brands report that the more complex issues are surfaced on Facebook because there are unlimited characters with which to describe them).

"There are a lot of brands in the U.S., even though they're investing in Social Customer Care [on] Twitter, kind of ignore Facebook," said March.

"The Marketing team might be doing stuff on it, maybe they moderate the public page, but otherwise they just don't think about it as a service channel in the same way." He added that Facebook's monetization model prioritizes transactions and promotions, so "they're not quite promoting the service use case even to consumers as heavily as Twitter."[13]

Internationally, the story is almost reversed, said March.

"It's a very different picture, partly because of the sheer scale of Facebook especially internationally compared to Twitter. And so if you go into Europe, you go into Asia Pac, you go into South America, suddenly there are countries where Twitter is far, far more smaller and pretty much all the Social Customer Care happening is happening through Facebook."[14]

Depending on your audience, providing Customer Service on LinkedIn, Instagram, Pinterest, Snapchat, WeChat, or other platforms may also be necessary.

If you are working in a regulated industry, there may be laws which require Customer Service to be available in any channel in which you are also marketing, but that's not a bad guideline regardless of industry.

Empowering Your Agents: Companies are often reluctant to truly empower their Customer Service agents to solve customer problems because of cost concerns. Customer Service expert Shep Hyken thinks this is a mistake:

"You've got to recognize there's a cost of doing business…And I think you have to be worried about what it will cost you if you don't handle things properly. But if you do it right and maybe once in a while it costs a little bit more, maybe a little more effort, maybe a little bit more time, maybe spend a little bit more money… that's the cost of doing business, that's the cost of staying in business."[15]

You can outline the extent to which your agents can act on behalf of a customer to solve a problem (creating the so-called "guardrails") when you develop your Process (See Chapter 8). For now, it is important to determine that this is indeed a priority.

Response Time: This is the time between the moment a customer posts a question or complaint to a brand, and the moment the brand first publicly acknowledges the post. As noted earlier, according to research conducted by Jay

Baer and Edison Research, among customers who expect a response in social media, nearly 40% expect that response within one hour. This number will certainly increase in the coming months and years. But here's the incredible part: Only 40% of social media complaints are addressed *at all*, and of those that are answered, the average response time is nearly five hours.[16] Clearly, "average" isn't good enough.

On the other side of the spectrum, Laurie Meacham, head of Social Customer Care for JetBlue, said that the airline's goal is a 10-minute response time.[17] The airline industry as a whole does tend to be best-in-class when it comes to response time, so if your goal is to be among the best of the best, you'll need to respond extremely fast. But not every industry needs to be held to that standard.

Consider an airline passenger who is standing in an airport after their flight has been abruptly canceled. There is a line 50 people deep to talk to the one Customer Service representative at the counter. That passenger, who decides to tweet at the airline, requires a response *now*, not in an hour, and certainly not in a day. Your customers, however, may not have the same sense of urgency when they have questions or concerns about your product or service. So listen to your customers to understand their response time expectations. If you don't know the answer, ask them!

It is also important to note that according to Twitter's own research, response time matters. A study of airline passengers who tweeted at airlines and received a response showed that they were willing to pay $9 more to the airline (for fees, snacks, etc.) after the experience. That number jumped to $20 when the response time was 6 minutes or less.[18]

"You're just not expecting someone to reach out and help you on a public medium like this," said Twitter researcher Wayne Huang. "There's definitely something that registers deep inside people's emotions, and they remember it and are willing to pay more for it."[19]

Customers who received responses from brands "felt overwhelmingly much more positive towards the brand" vs. those who did not receive a response. "Even just acknowledging someone's tweet, even if you can't solve it at that moment, that can really add a lot of value," Huang notes. "When you do respond, it's a strong social signal that [your brand] really takes customers very seriously... It takes just a few seconds, but it makes a huge difference."[20]

Further research went beyond the airline industry. Using conjoint analysis, Twitter also looked at tweets to and from national pizza delivery brands and telecom companies, and found that for pizza brands, customers were willing to spend $2.84 more (20%) after receiving a response from a brand on Twitter, while for telco companies it was $8.35 or 10%. In addition, responding faster increases the potential for additional revenue.[21]

Other SLAs (Service Level Agreement): Besides Response Time, you should determine at the outset what other SLAs you'll want to track and be accountable for. We'll discuss reporting in depth in Chapter 9, but for now let's consider a few more basic metrics:

1) *Resolution Time:* This is the time between the moment a customer posts a question or complaint to a brand, and the moment the brand resolves the customer's issue. Resolution Time, by definition, will always be equal to or longer than Response Time. Obviously, your goal should be to have as low of a Resolution Time as possible.

2) *Sentiment:* This is a reflection – usually expressed as Positive, Negative, and Neutral – of social opinion of your brand, based on public mentions. Part of your Social Customer Care Philosophy might be to improve the public perception of your brand through outstanding Customer Service, and sentiment analysis is a good way to measure against that goal.

3) *Traditional social media metrics:* Also known as "vanity metrics," these include Likes, Favorites, Comments, Retweets, and Shares. These metrics aren't just for marketers! Great Customer Service can help enhance and elevate the very metrics that social media marketers care about – usually at much lower cost – so they can become part of your Philosophy and goals, too.

When developing a Social Customer Care Philosophy, it's also important to consider the broad nature of your team's responsibilities as it relates to your company's products and services. Unlike telephone agents, who often have specialized knowledge that can be accessed through warm transfers or even an IVR (Interactive Voice Response) system, Social Customer Care agents often need to be a "jack of all trades."

Tweeters don't get to "choose 1 for account balance, 2 for recent payments." They tweet at a brand and expect a response, no matter the topic. This requires a different kind of agent – one who knows enough to be dangerous about nearly all facets of the company. They should be able to answer basic questions about all products and services, and know how to quickly obtain answers from other experts in the company for more complex questions. Of course, they should also understand the basics of social media.

Your existing Customer Service capabilities are also important to understand before starting a Social Customer Care program. Companies that are already great at Customer Service should not have trouble adding a new channel. But those who suffer from long hold times on the phone, unanswered emails, or unknowledgeable agents need to clean up the house first before bringing inferior service into the public eye.

PHILOSOPHY EXAMPLES

A good Social Customer Care Philosophy can be summarized much like a good 30-second "elevator pitch." Natanya Anderson, formerly of Whole Foods Market, described the Whole Foods Philosophy like this:

"I want people to have such great experiences with our Customer Care team that they want to tell other people about how great the care was, and then how much that makes them an advocate for Whole Foods Market."[22]

This is a bold goal! Make Social Customer Care so impactful that it causes your customers to tell other people about it and become an advocate for the brand. Social Customer Care can definitely be one of the most memorable experiences your customer has with your brand if you do it right.

Nicole Miller from Buffer looked at her company's Philosophy a little differently, but still very effectively: "We view every interaction that comes our way – every single tweet, email, question, mention – as a real privilege to know that someone has taken the time out of their day to think about us or get in touch with us."[23]

While not stated as a goal per se, Buffer's Social Customer Care Philosophy is easy to understand, because it puts the customer in the center, and it's inspirational to employees.

One of Telstra's television commercials boasts this claim: "We care about our customers. And we want to be famous for it."[24] Now that's something Telstra's employees can get excited about!

"In many ways, it's symbolic of our corporate strategy and that is very much [to be] an advocacy-first organization," said Monty Hamilton. "We believe that if we are able to create customer experiences and offer great products and services that have fair value, that our customers will keep coming back."[25]

You can also make your Philosophy more literal, such as this one aggregated from multiple brands:

We will strive to:
Serve our customers in the channel of their choice…
…24 hours a day, 7 days a week…
…with a best-in-class response time…
…addressing questions, compliments and complaints...
…in a personalized manner…
…keeping with our brand voice and personality.

Once you have your team's Philosophy written down, memorized, and socialized, you are ready for the next step.

5

TECHNOLOGY
(WINNING AT SOCIAL CUSTOMER CARE STEP #2)

Technology is the backbone that allows you to effectively scale your Social Customer Care efforts. Your program will only be as good as your technology allows it to be. It will "optimize the Customer Service experience and customer engagement workflow," according to Sparkcentral CEO Davy Kestens.[1]

That said, there are many different providers in the marketplace that offer a dizzying array of features. What's the best choice for your organization? This chapter will help you figure that out.

(Note: When I refer to the technology companies, I will call them "providers" whereas when I refer to the social media companies, I will call them "platforms.")

WHAT IS IT?

You may already be asking, "Why can't I just use the native social media platforms for Customer Service?" The answer is: You probably can, but only if you have very small volume. While the platforms themselves all have administrative portals that allow you to interact with people contacting your brand, they won't allow you to prioritize responses, assign them to multiple agents, track them for future use, report on metrics, or really much else. In addition, you'll have the burden of having to log in to each platform separately rather than having a unified queue of inquiries.

Most companies have realized the need for some technology above and beyond the native platforms in order to deliver consistently high levels of

Customer Service in social media. Still, it helps to understand the history a little bit.

"When Social Customer Care was just getting started, so many brands out there were making a ton of mistakes. Not a week would go by and there was some article bashing some company about them creating a really weird experience on social or saying the wrong things or posting the wrong photos," said Kestens. "You had brands double-responding to the same customer and then contradicting themselves… examples where a brand got hijacked because an employee quits but he still had the root password of the Twitter account.

"It became rather obvious that there wasn't really any level of oversight or compliance or control within those organizations on how to handle social, especially given it was run by the Marketing department from Day One."[2]

Rob Hahn of Southwest Airlines said the company knew it was time to shift Social Customer Care to the Customer Service team when customers started responding to Marketing posts with service inquiries.

"They started airing questions, also complaints about their travel experience so our Marketing Communications team did an awesome job assisting those customers but they were still having to come to Customer Relations to get all the details to help these customers," he said. "Back in 2011, we partnered with Marketing Communications and decided, 'hey let's start a Social Customer Care team' and because our team has all the tools to serve these customers, let's start a team within that group to serve these customers."[3]

Conversocial CEO Joshua March saw the same opportunity, noting that enterprise Customer Service vendors weren't able "to innovate fast enough to stay up to date with social." He suggests companies start with this question: "How can you use technology as a tool to make your customers' lives and your agents' lives agents better, but still deliver that kind of humanity at scale and make sure it doesn't get in the way and become just another kind of cranky IVR system that your customers are going to hate and end up not using?"[4]

OK, so that may have been several questions wrapped up into one, but they were good questions! How can technology make your customers' lives easier? How can it make your agents' lives easier? And how can it allow the brand to remain human in a channel that demands it?

"We're able to leverage technology to help keep us streamlined and really focused on the customer experience," said Michelle Mattson of T-Mobile. "I think it's really important for people to look at technology and leverage it in ways that allow you to be agile, flexible and move quickly."[5]

Indeed, according to Conversocial's *Definitive Guide*, "A viable solution turns the chaos and noise of social media chatter into streamlined threads and queues that are easy to manage and ensure best in class Customer Service."[6]

WHAT DO YOU NEED TO THINK ABOUT?

There are several things you need to think about when looking at the technology that will support your Social Customer Care program.

An "all-in-one" provider vs. dedicated service provider: An "all-in-one" provider is designed with both publishing capabilities for the Marketing team and servicing capabilities for the Customer Service team. A dedicated service provider is only for Customer Service. There are pros and cons of each, discussed below.

Investment: Like with most purchase decisions, you can buy the base-model Buick or the souped-up Lexus. For the most part, you'll get what you pay for; the more expensive providers offer a wider variety of features and functionality, and if you choose to separate the publishing and Customer Service providers you'll likely pay a bit more overall. But your business may not need all the bells and whistles, so consider your individual needs both now and, importantly, in the future. It's OK to "grow into" the technology; the selection process can be arduous so make sure you choose wisely the first time.

Platform Integrations: You'll want to know which social media platforms the technology supports. Some only support Facebook and Twitter; others have added Instagram, Pinterest, LinkedIn, and others. Do you need ratings and review sites or external communities included? What about messaging platforms like WhatsApp or WeChat? Make sure the provider can handle them and that it stays up-to-date as new platforms emerge.

Sparkcentral's Kestens said the rapidly expanding world of social media is the pain point that often causes companies to seek technology help.

"Quite often it's like, 'Help we're freaking out. Marketing opened this random (insert new channel) and now customers are asking us questions about service,'" he said.

But he also warns that channels may someday become irrelevant.

"How can we make it easy for the customer and how do we enable brands to talk to customers across any channel?'" he asks. "Because really it's not about the channel, it's about the customer."[7]

It's also important to ask about the quality of the integration, because not all integrations are the same. Facebook and Twitter both have "preferred providers" that often receive special access to data, or perhaps more frequent pinging (the number of times the provider can access the social media platform's server to download new posts and data).

Language Support: Obviously this is only relevant if you are offering Customer Service in more than one language. You'll want to know how many languages are supported, whether more are in the works, whether any sort of translation service comes with the package, and how the technology recognizes foreign languages. Some languages, such as Turkish, are much harder to identify and interpret than more common languages like Spanish, so if you have a special language need make sure you ask about it.

Workflow Options: This "enables you to add a layer of automation, providing a smart workflow for large-scale Customer Service teams, and empowering your agents to deliver better and faster social Customer Service," according to Conversocial's *Definitive Guide*.[8] In other words, the software acts like an automated IVR (Interactive Voice Response) system on the back end, routing inquires to the right agent but without the annoying "Press 1 for Sales, Press 2 for Service" options presented to the customer.

Technical Support: Ironically, this is about the Customer Service that your Customer Service provider provides. What is the process for contacting the provider when the technology is not working? Are they available 24 hours a day, 7 days a week? How long does it normally take to resolve technical problems? Are you going to be charged for technical support or is it included in your base price? Will you have a dedicated support team or do you have to call a toll-free number and hope for the best? Is on-site technical support available or is it always remote? These are all questions you'll want to ask *before* you have a technical glitch!

Strategic Support: This is a different kind of service. This is about the openness of the provider to listen to your Philosophy, goals and needs, and customize the technology accordingly. Providers will often assign someone to your account (the person may or may not be dedicated) who will set up regular calls with you to check in, problem solve, and take product enhancement requests back to the Development team. Since every industry is different, you'll want to be clear with any expectations that might be unique to your company. Examples include: Is there a field in the software for a loyalty number? Can the provider integrate with your CRM? Can the provider make changes to their physical or data security policies to align with your company's rules for vendors?

Innovation Roadmap: You don't want to partner with a technology company that is standing still. Not only should the provider be able to demonstrate a quick reaction time to the constantly upgraded functionality on the major social media platforms (such as Facebook introducing quick links to Messenger and Messenger Bots, or Twitter someday extending the character length of tweets), but the company should also have a robust innovation roadmap of its own which includes new features to make your and your team's job easier and the customer experience better. There should also be an openness to allowing you, their loyal customer, to impact the roadmap.

THREE DIFFERENT TYPES OF TECHNOLOGY

In general, there are three types of Customer Service providers in the marketplace, ranging from pretty basic to incredibly sophisticated. As you move from one to the next, you'll most likely see an increase in cost, features and functionality, as well as Customer Service expertise.

Free/Mass Subscriptions: These are websites that are available to the general public, often with limited functionality for free and a premium version for a modest monthly or annual fee. They can be used for most individuals and some small companies, but their functionality is going to be comparatively basic. Expect to be able to separate posts into multiple streams, based on keywords, hashtags, and/or brand mentions. You can also post to social media platforms either immediately or via a personalized schedule, which saves time and effort for Marketing posts but isn't really useful for Customer Service replies. Examples of Free/Mass Subscriptions include: Buffer, Hootsuite, Sprout Social, and Twitter's own TweetDeck.

All-In-One Enterprise Solutions: These are subscription-based providers aimed at medium- to large-size companies which are looking to consolidate publishing and Customer Service into a single platform. The thing to remember about these types of solutions – and this is neither an endorsement nor a condemnation of any of them – is that they typically started as publishing-only providers until they realized the demand for Customer Service capabilities. If you are making the technology decision alongside your Marketing team, they will immediately and understandably lean toward one of these solutions because publishing is still what all-in-one's do best.

That said, over the past few years the All-In-One power players have spent considerable resources to bulk up the Customer Service portion of their offerings. This includes features such as queueing rules and the ability to see an entire customer conversation, even if it spans weeks or months. (This is called "threading" conversations, and it's ideal that the software can integrate both public and private messages on the same social platform into the same "thread." As of this writing, I don't know of any system that can integrate across social media platforms – in other words, connecting the conversations of the same person on Facebook and Twitter, for example – but I'm pretty sure some company will eventually figure that out, too.)

For many companies, an all-in-one solution is absolutely a terrific option. Expect to pay either a flat monthly or annual rate or a per-seat license that can quickly eclipse six figures annually. Examples of All-in-One Enterprise Solutions include: Adobe, Percolate, Salesforce, Spredfast, and Sprinklr.

Dedicated Customer Service Providers: This is software that was built from the ground up to handle Customer Service, and only Customer Service. The providers do not claim to be publishing platforms, nor is it advisable to use them as such. The way these providers have approached Customer Service in social media is by creating an experience that will be recognizable to call center employees and leadership.

"As I spent time in these contact centers, I started to realize that to bridge that gap between this rapidly shifting world of social and the needs of this large scale contact center environment was a really big task, and it wasn't a task that I thought would be possible to complete if you're also trying to meet all the needs of the Marketing department in terms of campaign management [and] advertising," said Conversocial's Joshua March, of his decision to focus his software exclusively on Customer Service.[9]

In contrast to the all-in-one providers which had to add a Customer Service offering to existing publishing software, the dedicated service platforms have the advantage of building exclusively for Customer Service. The result is a more holistic Customer Service offering that truly has all the bells and whistles.

The Conversocial *Definitive Guide* lays out the case for a Dedicated Service Provider:

"Marketing is making the majority of decisions when it comes to Social Media. This often results in a disconnect between Customer Service and Marketing, with the former stuck using Social Media Management Suites (SMMS) for Customer Service. These suites are often great for Marketing but insufficient for the complex needs of a Customer Service department.

"Ultimately, dedicated solutions allow Customer Service teams to do what they do best—serve the customer. These teams are not focused on reaching as many people as possible, building brand awareness or adding subscribers like their Marketing colleagues, and as such require a different tool."[10]

If you invite some Social Customer Care agents to the provider demonstrations (which is a best practice), they will most likely relate to the dedicated Customer Service providers the best because the process will seem most familiar. That's the advantage; the disadvantage, of course, is that you'll need to purchase two different solutions, one for publishing and one for service. This will not only cause eye rolling in your IT department, but it's almost assuredly going to cost more than a single solution. Expect to pay either a flat monthly or annual rate or a per-seat license that will definitely be six figures annually once you include both providers. Examples of Dedicated Customer Service Providers include: Brand Embassy, Conversocial, Lithium, and Sparkcentral.

WHICH IS THE BEST SOLUTION FOR YOU?

There are several considerations that will help determine the answer to this question. Budget is, of course, one of them. A couple hundred thousand dollars is a lot more money for some companies than for others. It's also important to lean back on your Social Customer Care Philosophy; at a previous employer our goal was to be "world-class" in Social Customer Care because we believed we were already there in other Customer Service channels. In order to be "world-class," we felt like we needed a world-class Customer Service platform (and, for that matter, a world-class publishing platform) so we went with the dual provider model. Interestingly, the all-in-one provider who was awarded the contract was actually disappointed that they "only" received the publishing portion.

Your Philosophy may not include being "world-class" in Social Customer Care, and that's absolutely fine. Maybe you just want to address complaints in social media before they become public relations problems. Maybe the volume of interactions your company is receiving is just too small to warrant a large investment of technology. Maybe you are a team of one answering all customer inquiries yourself, so added functionality that allows multiple agents and complicated queueing strategies is wholly unnecessary.

Other things you may want to think about when making this important decision:

Collision Avoidance: Do you require that multiple agents be able to use the software concurrently and not "collide" with each other? When several users are handling inquiries at the same time, it is important that they be able to "claim" a post as theirs while they are researching an answer and eventually responding, so that the same customer doesn't inadvertently receive multiple responses to the same question.

Prioritization: Do you need your social media posts prioritized in any personalized manner? The default for most providers – as well as for the social media platforms themselves – is reverse chronological order. That's also the most intuitive format for most people, and many companies prefer the "first in, first out" approach of responding, but some companies may want to prioritize responses based on other factors. These can include: the elite loyalty program status of the poster; the number of posts in the current discussion string; the social media influence of the poster (as judged by services such as Klout or Klear or even just number of followers); the urgency or negativity of the post (measured via language or sentiment analysis); certain keywords included in the post, or perhaps the location of the poster or time of day/night that the post was received.

Companies may also want some messages *de-prioritized*, such as spam or other un-actionable posts, auto-generated posts, and messages with similar spellings (we had a lot of challenges separating "Discover" from the verb "discover").

Reporting: What types of reporting will you require? We'll cover reporting more deeply in Chapter 9, but for now you'll want to determine the frequency of your desired reporting and the broad types of reporting that you'll need. Some providers can create personalized reports in real-time, while others use a batch system that may occur overnight.

"Real-time analytics are key to continually monitoring the SLA and KPI [Key Performance Indicator] attainment of agents," according to the Conversocial *Definitive Guide*. This can include "historical insights into trends over time to deliver actionable insight for your business."[11] If you're going to want to see separate reporting by agent or call center location, this is the time to request that.

Technology "empowers our people to do a fantastic job, it gives them an understanding of how many inquiries they're responding to, understanding the sentiment of how customers feel about those inquiries," said Telstra's Monty Hamilton. "It really is a liberation moment for organizations."[12]

Security: Are there specific security or regulatory considerations that your company has? "Look for a software that provides role-based permissions, an approval workflow, IP locking and a fully searchable, exportable archive," suggests the Conversocial *Definitive Guide*.[13] These capabilities are critical to ensuring only the right people have access to post on the brand's behalf, new agents are properly trained before answering live customer inquiries, and any customer interaction can be easily retrieved if a compliance question arises or a government agency requests it.

CRM Integration: Will you require integration with an existing CRM system? We'll talk more about this in Chapter 11, but right now you'll need to ask if the provider integrates with your CRM system currently or, if not, whether they are willing to build that connection for you. "It is vital to choose a social Customer Service software with a full set of APIs, which allows you to surface social information through your CRM systems and contact center technologies," notes the Conversocial *Definitive Guide*.[14]

Contract: What kind of contract style(s) does your company prefer? Providers can charge flat fees or a "seat license," which is essentially a per-user fee. Contracts can be inclusive of technological and strategic support services, or those services may create additional hourly charges. Make sure that expectations are clearly laid out at the beginning so there are no financial surprises.

Speed to Market: How quickly do you need to launch? With added product complexity often comes added installation complexity. Don't just listen to what the provider salespeople say (because they'll all tell you it's incredibly easy); ask your IT, Security, Risk, and Legal departments as well and have them connect with their counterparts at the vendor before you sign a contract.

Whichever type of provider you choose, it is strongly advisable that you go through a formal RFP (Request For Proposal) process. Although this process can often be time-consuming, it is important that you not chase the first "shiny object" you see when it comes to technology selection. Make sure the right people are in the room evaluating vendors together – Customer Service agents and leadership, Marketing, IT, the CRM team, and if necessary, someone from Legal, Compliance, and/or Security. Spend the time to compare and contrast features, service, and fees, and don't be afraid to negotiate on price once you have several offers in hand. Larger companies will have a Procurement team that can lead this process and provide a scorecard for all participants.

The decision you make here will impact your Social Customer Care program for years to come, so don't underestimate its importance.

6

TEAM SELECTION
(WINNING AT SOCIAL CUSTOMER CARE STEP #3)

While it is critical to have an inspiring Social Customer Care Philosophy and the right technology, no Social Customer Care program can be successful without the right people interacting with your customers and prospects. The hiring of the front-line Social Customer Care staff should be thoughtful, strategic, and intentional, as it will set up the rest of the program to be able to scale in the future.

What complicates this part of the process is that the Social Customer Care agents will likely report up through an Operations or Customer Service division, whereas you as a social media leader may be part of the Marketing or Communications team. Customer Service will likely already have a robust hiring process in place; it is important for you to respect that process but also to introduce some additional steps that will ensure the right kind of agent behind the proverbial wheel.

WHAT DO YOU NEED TO LOOK FOR?
The first question people usually ask when thinking about hiring for a Social Customer Care team is whether they should prioritize Customer Service experience or social media prowess. Of course it is preferable that candidates have both, but if you must choose then the choice is clear: It is much easier to teach social media skills than it is to teach someone how to care for a customer.

The patience, empathy, compassion and friendliness that a Customer Service agent must possess to be successful are extremely difficult to teach.

Remember the person at the fast-food restaurant who seemed to consider you an interruption or a burden? What are the chances that you'd be able to train that person to genuinely care about each and every customer as if they were family?

Customer Service Consultant John R. DiJulius III calls this skill "Service Aptitude," which is critical to have in every single employee of your company, he said. In his book, *What's The Secret?: To Providing a World-Class Customer Experience*, DiJulius defines "Service Aptitude" as: "A person's ability to recognize opportunities to exceed Customers' expectations, regardless of the circumstances."[1]

Michelle Mattson of T-Mobile looks for candidates who "demonstrate a passion for customer experience."[2]

Just because someone is good at social media doesn't mean they know the first thing about how to treat your customers. Sure, it helps if the candidate is active on Facebook and Twitter and understands the nuances of hashtags and DMs, but the mechanics of the various social media platforms can be taught; empathy cannot.

The first step is writing a solid job description. Again, you may have to start from an existing Customer Service job description, but that's OK. Generally the types of skills that are found in a telephone, email, or chat agents are transferrable to Social Customer Care. But you'll need to tweak it a bit and add a few more requirements. Specifically:

Writing Skills: These are a must. Social Customer Care agents must be able to communicate effectively with the written word, more so because much of the communication will be public. These public responses are a reflection of your brand, so you don't want them littered with spelling and grammar errors or sentences that don't make sense.

"You better have good grammar," said Mattson, listing that as one of the top required qualifications of agents who join her team. "Please don't tweet a weird version of your/you're, there/their – that drives me nuts. So writing is key."[3]

Make sure you require at least one writing sample as part of the candidate application.

Writing in 140 Characters: Twitter writing skills are even better. Writing on Twitter is a slightly different skill than writing in other forums. Remember when your high school English teacher told you to "write tight"? She probably explained that it was important to eliminate really superfluous words that needlessly extended your already lengthy sentences even more than they had to be just so you sounded more intelligent to those reading your paper and filled up the entire page with words and... well you get the point!

This is a critical skill on Twitter given its limitation of 140 characters per tweet. (Note: If Twitter ever decides to extend the character length, which I suspect they will even though I'd personally vote against it, tight writing skills will still be important, albeit less so.) Even in Facebook, it is important for Customer Service agents to get to the point quickly, not waste the customer's time, and not say more than what needs to be said. If the candidate is not active on Twitter, look for related skills like journalism (especially headline writing), copy editing, advertising copy writing, or SMS marketing.

Social Media Experience: While being active on social media is not required, it definitely helps. People who frequently use social media platforms have an inherent sense for how each of them work. They know what a hashtag is, and that one or two is ideal on Twitter but many more are acceptable on Instagram and despite Facebook's efforts, not many people use them there.

Perhaps most importantly, people active on social media understand the importance of the "social" in social media – that it's about the conversation and engagement with people, not the brand shouting its message with a megaphone.

Ideally, you or someone on the Social Media team can also be one of the interviewers for each candidate. If left to the Customer Service team to interview alone, the key components listed above likely won't get prioritized. For example, they may not be used to reading and reacting to writing samples or asking about social media experience. Another benefit of the social media team participating in the hiring process is that it forces collaboration with Customer Service. Now both groups will have an incentive to hire the right people for these critical roles.

What are some other things you should look for when interviewing prospective candidates? "Passion is huge," said James Degnan, community support manager at Xbox, which holds the *Guinness Book of World Records* title of "Most Responsive Brand on Twitter"[4]. "You have to have a strong ability to multi-task. Being passionate for the brand or Twitter really helps. And being able to demonstrate empathy & critical problem solving skills are a must."[5]

The Conversocial *Definitive Guide* suggests that great social Customer Service agents should also:

Be personable: During the interview process, assess whether this person can actually hold a conversation about a particular issue.

Be confident: A great social Customer Service agent must have the confidence to trust their instincts to quickly assess the context of a message and then be able to take the appropriate action.

Be curious: It is essential that social Customer Service agents have the eagerness not only to learn new tools but also to know the industry inside-out.

Be resilient: No matter the context, social agents must be able to react calmly, assess a situation and respond back to the customer. They must be able to show not only patience, but an ability to 'roll with the punches' by responding professionally in any scenario.[6]

In his book, *The Customer Service Revolution*, John R. DiJulius III suggests incorporating the "5 E's" into your interview process, counting the number of times a candidate displays each of the items. The "5 E's" are:

1. Eye contact was made
2. Ear-to-ear smiles took place
3. Enthusiasm was displayed
4. Engagement with the interview occurred naturally
5. Educated answers to interview questions were explored thoroughly[7]

INTERNAL OR EXTERNAL?

Laurie Meacham of JetBlue said she only hires internally, which ensures knowledge of, and passion for, the brand. "We want them to have a solid understanding of who JetBlue is as a brand," she said, "and they have to have a dual ability to think about things through a PR [Public Relations] lens as well as a customer support lens."[8]

The PR point should be obvious but is often overlooked; since social media is public, teams need to be cognizant of the fact that everything they write can be seen by someone else and is therefore a reflection of the brand. PR skills also come in handy during a crisis situation, when an issue gets emotionally escalated and shared many times across multiple channels.

According to Conversocial's *Definitive Guide*, "On social, agents become brand ambassadors and therefore need to possess all the skills that come with a public-facing role, on top of the abilities needed to be a great agent over traditional channels like phone and email."[9]

Southwest's Rob Hahn also looks inside the company for qualified candidates.

"We've been hiring from within our Customer Relations department," he said. "We found so many great perks from doing that because these folks have already been trained on our policies so they know our policies in and out. They've been trained on either corresponding with customers over the telephone or via email. So they already know how to talk to our customers. Now it's just layering on training on how to use our social tools and then how our social voice reads online."[10]

Here's how the Conversocial *Definitive Guide* weighs in on the issue of internal vs. external hires:

"Is it best to promote agents internally or to hire new agents for social? While great agents can come from both sources, we generally recommend promoting from within whenever possible for the following reasons:

1) You are able to identify agents who already have both strong writing skills and a great rapport with customers
2) The agents will already be familiar with your core contact center operations, allowing you to focus on social training

3) Joining the social team should be a reward for excellent work. Social agents are typically seen as the 'elite' team within the contact center

4) Since social Customer Service is a relatively young field, there is currently a very small pool of agents that have social on their resume, giving outside recruitment little advantage."[11]

Scott Wise of Scotty's Brewhouse said he looks for "emotional intelligence" when hiring staff. "It's not IQ, it's EQ, it's that emotional quotient where you *get* people. You understand. You're empathetic. And you *know* – you just know in your being what they [customers] want and what they need. And you bring it to them, and they're just like, 'Wow, this place actually gets it.'"[12]

If it sounds like he's saying, "I just know it when I see it," it's because he's had plenty of practice. So how does he actually know?

"If somebody says they've worked three years at Ruth's Chris Steak House, I tell them, 'Guess what? I don't give two [bleeps] where you've worked because I can teach anybody how to serve a burger and fries and get the temperature right, and get a drink out to somebody.' What I want to know is, tell me the best joke you heard in the last three days!

"We hire for smiles and we train for talent. So I want to hire you because you looked me in the eye when you walked into the interview and that I can count how many teeth you have because you smiled several times and that you had a personality that jumped off the page at me. So that's what we train our team to look for because that's the stuff that you can't teach. When you come to me at the age of 21 years old and you're looking for a job to serve, I can't teach you the things that are becoming lost arts in our world. How to say please and thank you and open the door for somebody and pull a chair out for somebody. I think these are the lost arts of such a simple way to make an incredible impact on someone. It's not Customer Service. It's just good manners. It's just having a good polite person to work for you."[13]

Amy Bivin, manager of community outreach for Dell, looks for candidates with varied backgrounds so they can help solve many types of problems.

Bivin's background in technical support, quality auditing, and executive escalations has helped her adapt to social media Customer Service, and she has hired other agents with similarly complementary skills.

"Those were really great skills and experiences to have," she said. "It empowered us with the knowledge and the ability and the tools to be able to resolve just about any problem that Dell hears about from our customers."[14]

Customer Service expert Shep Hyken told a story about his first job on the *Focus on Customer Service* podcast that epitomizes the type of person we should all be looking to hire:

"I worked at a gas station that I'll never forget. I was actually in college working at this gas station. But one very, very cold day perhaps one of the coldest days on record in St. Louis, Missouri where I live, a woman got out of the car to pump gas, an elderly woman. I don't know how old she was – 80, 85… I went out and pumped her for gas for her. My manager got upset with me for pumping this lady's gas. He says, 'we're a self-serve station' and I thought, well you know but she could have died, slipped on a piece of ice, I mean she looked frail. So I helped her and he says, 'What is she going to do the next time? She's going expect the same thing.' And I go, 'Well that's fine because there's three other stations, one on each of the corners at the intersection, and I think that I'd love her to come back and always do business with us.'"[15]

Wise also told a story about one of his employees that captures the essence of the "emotional intelligence" he talked about earlier:

"I had a server [who] was listening to his table talk and they said they've got to wrap up and they wished they could spend more time together but the meter was running out. And the server didn't even tell me this. The guest actually sent me this email. And he said, 'I've just got to tell you, this kid heard us talking about that, and he took change out of his own pocket and went out and put it in my car and came back and said, 'Hey you guys take more time, I went ahead and fed your meter, you're good.' ' … It literally chokes me up because that's the kind of stuff that you can't teach somebody."[16]

ORGANIZATIONAL STRUCTURE

It's very important to determine early on where Social Customer Care will sit in the organization. Generally, it starts in the Marketing department because that's where the Social Media team sits. But more often than not, Marketing folks are more interested in outbound messaging than dealing with customer inquiries.

"In the early days…almost every company that was getting into this space had a very specific social team," said Conversocial's Joshua March. "Social is this very new thing and companies were setting up these dedicated teams that usually came out of Marketing or were a part of Marketing and we worked with a lot of these social teams who had just been focusing on the outbound publishing side of things.

"We were starting to realize that they needed to get Customer Service involved and we would often work with them at about that time and help them take social into the customer center, get real customer agents responding and enable them to actually start resolving issues at scale."[17]

So the Social Customer Care team should ideally sit in the Customer Service department. And indeed, Sparkcentral's Davy Kestens said that today, "75 percent of our customers live in a contact center."[18]

"Your current call center director – although the technology may be a bit antiquated – will understand the intricacies of Customer Service far better than any marketer," notes Sparkcentral's *7 Steps* white paper. "The reality is, your Marketing team is simply not an expert in all facets of social media… [they're] not experts in supporting your particular product or service... which is vital."[19]

But in large companies the Customer Service team can be huge, with thousands (or tens of thousands) of agents in multiple locations. Do not let the Social Customer Care team – destined in almost all companies except startups to be tiny compared to the team dedicated to phone service – get lost in the shuffle or put in the proverbial corner ("Nobody puts Social Customer Care in the corner!").

Ideally, the Social Customer Care team will operate as an independent unit with a generalized skill set. In other words, they will know enough to be dangerous about virtually every part of the business. (This will require strong training, as discussed in Chapter 7.)

In the telephone world, agents have the luxury of being specialized thanks to automatic routing systems that can transfer a customer to the "right" agent based on the reason they are calling. While this is technically possible in social media (depending on the technology provider you select), it is generally not advised except for maybe the largest of companies because it adds to response time and/or resolution time. The time you spend triaging a complaint (determining which department it should be routed to and sending it to a specialist) is better spent responding immediately and beginning to engage the customer with either a high-level answer or a request to take the conversation offline.

The main advantage of the Social Customer Care team being "independent" is that it will prevent the resource management team from transferring Social Customer Care agents to the telephone when phone volumes increase. This is a typical call center reaction – to prioritize the telephone over all other channels – but it results in a horrible customer experience for digitally-minded customers. No one wants to wait days for an email response, or see the "Live Chat Not Available" sign on the website, or be ignored in social media. If your company's goal is truly to service the customer in the channel of *their* choice (vs. the channel of *your* choice), then you need to staff appropriately – and independently – in every channel.

That being said, operational efficiency is a key goal of most call centers and should be a key goal of a Social Customer Care team, too. If you do not have enough volume in social media to warrant full-time staff, then it is definitely a best practice to cross-train agents on at least one other digital channel. I suggest email because the fact is, customer expectations of email response time (usually 24-48 hours) are much more manageable, creating obvious prioritization rules.

Since social media originated in the Marketing department, it is important to keep the lines of communication open between Marketing and Customer Service. (Incidentally, this is good advice for any Customer Service channel, not just social.) The Sparkcentral *7 Steps* white paper suggests that you "develop a liaison between your marketing and Customer Service team. Make sure there is an ongoing dialogue – paying close attention to who is 'listening' to what channel."[20]

Also keep in mind that the goals of Marketing and Customer Service are different, but ideally they are complementary. The Conversocial *Definitive Guide* spells out the differing priorities this way[21]:

Marketing Priorities:
Gathering customer data
Increase conversion rates
Building brand awareness
Digital measurement
Growth from new subscribers

Customer Service Priorities:
Scalability and efficiency
Managing risk
Building an awe-inspiring experience
Associate development
Growth from existing customers

Every company structure is different; some are simpler and others are more complicated. Find out how a few other companies are organized and that will give you good ideas for what makes the most sense for your company.

Allison Leahy of Fitbit explained her company's organizational structure during a *Focus on Customer Service* podcast episode:

"We are a global team all under the umbrella of the Community team which is within the Customer Support department. We're currently operating out of five locations and at the heart of our work are our customer advocates and community advocates; these are the folks on the front lines responding to all of your toughest tweets, your funny Facebook posts, and reviews published to Amazon or iTunes.

"We also have a second tier of advocate, a more tenured group who is helping out with some of the real-time queue management and floor support to ensure that as our product line diversifies and we release more products and those products become more complicated, that we have all the information we need on the front lines to get your questions answered as quickly and efficiently as possible. And that group also helps out with other assignments like marketing campaign support or new product launches when some of the questions we might receive are unanticipated.

"Coaching and managing the daily workflow of these advocates are our team leads. And we also have dedicated customer experience analysts who audit a few interactions per advocate per week to ensure that all our proper communication guidelines and procedures are followed. We also have operations managers who oversee the team leads and customer experience analysts and collaborate more closely with workforce management who help us out to ensure staffing is in place and all of our KPIs are being met."[22]

Duke Energy, the largest utility in the United States, has a unique organizational strategy: The Social Customer Care team is co-located with the Corporate Communications team and they "share the channels."

"Things can change really quickly," said Madeleine Piercy, social media strategist for Duke Energy. "A customer interaction can become a brand reputation action really quickly." As the team figures out how to scale, they're leaning on call center people who have knowledge of the business and are "teaching them social."[23]

INCENTIVE STRUCTURES

Most call centers incentivize their agents based on traditional telephone service metrics. You should determine if the metrics that your call center agents are judged on will translate to social media or not. For some metrics, like First Call Resolution, you might just have to tweak the name of the metric (I love the concept of "First Tweet Resolution"). Others, like Average Handle Time (AHT) or Customer Satisfaction (CSAT), will have direct ties to social media Customer Service as well.

But some metrics, like call abandonment rate (the number of customers who give up because of busy signals or long hold times) may not have a direct correlation to social media. Just make sure that your Social Customer Care agents have the same ability to earn bonuses or other rewards as their telephone counterparts, without completely re-writing your company's incentive structure.

SCALING

Be ready for your Social Customer Care team to grow quickly as volumes increase in traditional social media platforms as well as newer messaging platforms. Southwest's Rob Hahn experienced this first-hand.

"Back in 2014, at the beginning of the year we had four representatives managing all this," he said. "Now we have 32 representatives and three leaders so 2015 has been an amazing year for us to experience all that growth."[24]

Your company may not experience 8X growth in less than two years, but it will certainly grow as you get good at responding to online customer inquiries and your customers learn that social media is a fast, easy, and helpful channel from which to get answers.

If your business is seasonal, be sure to prepare ahead of time for seasonal surges which will require additional manpower. For example, Piercy's Social Customer Care team at Duke Energy has to be prepared for a rapid onslaught of inquiries in the event of inclement weather.

"We're very weather based, so if there's a storm we need to ramp up really quickly and respond," she said. "But then if it's blue sky and the weather's good, we might not hear from a lot of people."[25]

The Sparkcentral *7 Steps* white paper suggests that you "know your business and try to anticipate and plan for seasonal business surges… Don't be caught off guard – make sure you can maintain the same quality of service whether you're receiving 40 tweets a day or 4,000… be nimble enough to scale up or scale down, depending on your current needs as well as preparing for the foreseeable future."[26]

Even as you scale, don't cut corners when hiring for Customer Service, because it's too important. This is your company's "front line" – often the only employees your customers will ever talk to – so they have enormous power to influence the overall customer experience.

"You're hiring for Customer Service, hire the right person," said Hyken. "Don't make a mistake, do it right, get the right people. And that means a painstakingly thorough interview or sets of interviews and behavioral style testing. But if you get the right person in there to start with, you're going to be better at what you do… And even if you have to pay that person a little bit more, long term this person pays off."[27]

Training
(Winning at Social Customer Care Step #4)

Once you've hired the right people to be the face of your Social Customer Care program to your customers, it's time to train them. Once again, your training may overlap with existing Customer Service training in your organization, but there will need to be some added elements that are specific to Social Customer Care because as we discussed earlier, social media is a unique channel in a lot of ways.

Conversocial's *Definitive* Guide points out three major differences between social media and other Customer Service channels, creating new challenges for agents. Social media is[1]:

Noisy: Unlike other channels, agents must sift through a lot of content in order to identify Customer Service issues on social.

Confusing: Multiple public and private messages from a single customer are hard to track, and can get lost between agents.

High Stakes: A single error can result in a full-blown social media crisis.

Specifically, you'll want to focus your training on your core business, your Social Customer Care Philosophy, your technology, Customer Service best practices, and social media platforms.

YOUR CORE BUSINESS

As noted earlier, social Customer Service agents often need to be a "jack of all trades." Unlike many other Customer Service agents who may be able to specialize in one area of the business, your Social Customer Care agents will need to act as "super-agents" – knowing at least a little bit about every part of the business, and knowing whom to call when the questions get especially complex. (Note: In very large companies, your Technology platform should be able to help manage this, allowing you to have more experts than generalists.) I would argue that this is a good skill to impart to all employees in an organization, not just Customer Service agents. I constantly encourage my teams to learn about other areas of the business by:

- Attending internal town halls where multiple areas of the business are presenting
- Signing up for training classes to extend knowledge of the company and industry
- Scheduling coffee meetings with people in different areas of the company
- Finding opportunities to work cross-functionally on a project with other groups in the company
- Listening to Customer Service calls regularly
- Scrolling through the company's social media feeds to find out what the company is talking about and what its customers are talking about
- Reading press articles about the company
- If your company is publicly traded, listening to earnings calls – both the company's presentation and the analysts' questions

While you don't need your Social Customer Care agents to do all of the above, some of these steps will be very helpful. Mostly, though, you'll want to quickly expose them to the company's products and services, preferably with leaders from different business units presenting live and answering questions afterward. You'll also want to give them an overview of your industry and direct competitors, as many Customer Service inquiries will compare your company's product or service to that of a competitor. While it's generally not a best practice to talk about your competitors in social media, it is critical that your Social Customer Care agents understand how your offerings are different than competitors' offerings, and how to talk about those differences publicly.

Agents should also understand their role within the larger Customer Service organization and the larger company. Inviting a Customer Experience speaker to present to a new class of agents can help explain the importance of their role as front-line employees in shaping a customer's overall opinion of the brand. It can also help communicate a consistent brand voice across all service channels.

When training on brand voice, it is also important to teach agents that they should try to put themselves in customers' shoes. That's more than empathy; in social media, it's also responding in a similar tone and style as the customer (when appropriate), to establish a more personal connection.

Discover did that with its spot-on response to the somewhat sarcastic customer asking about "persistence or lack of coordination." Similarly, T-Mobile's Michelle Mattson said she tries to teach new agents, "How do you respond to a customer who's being a smart ass and match that without really stepping out of bounds?"[2]

Of course, as we discussed in the last chapter, there are some things you simply can't teach. "Years ago I read a great quote by [Bruce] Nordstrom who [was] asked, 'How do you train people to be so good at a Nordstrom department store?'" recalls Customer Service expert Shep Hyken. "And he said, 'We don't train them; their parents train them.'"[3]

Scott Wise addresses this dilemma by providing each of his employees with a card containing the company's vision, which is based on the classic book, *All I Really Need to Know I Learned in Kindergarten* by Robert Fulghum.

"On the front of the card, I put the statement: 'I will act in a way that will make my _____ proud.' We hand these out to every person who gets hired in our company and I let them fill that out. I said, 'You don't have to come to work to make me proud. If you want to make yourself or your parents or you've got a child or a husband or a wife then just act in a way that you're going to make somebody proud.'

"The [inside of the] card just has about 20 different things that really in my opinion encompasses what we're all about… These are the qualities you can't teach."[4]

Be nice. | Share. | Be polite. Remember your manners. Say: Please, Thank You, I'm Sorry. | Open doors for people. Pull chairs out for people. Smile and laugh. | Put things back where you found them. Clean up your own mess. | Don't take things that aren't yours. Don't hit. Play fair. | Flush. Wash your hands. | Milk, cookies and Dill Chips are good for you. | Learn, think, work & play, every day. | When someone falls, help them up. At work. In life. In our world. | Give one person a compliment every. single. day. | Be passionate about something. Make a difference. Leave a mark. | Trying and making a mistake is better than not trying at all. | Learn from your mistakes. Don't make the same one twice. | Help someone cross the street. Especially when no one is looking. | Every 90 days, do some kind of charity work: donate time, mind & soul. | Hold hands & stick together. We are a team and family. United.

MOST FREQUENT INQUIRY TYPES

In most companies, the same questions emerge over and over again in Customer Service. Your company's website or community forum should contain the answers to these questions so customers who are willing to self-serve can find them, but there will always be people who just find it easier to ask someone than to search for it themselves. (This reminds me of a hilarious website called "Let Me Google That For You" that creates a link you can share with someone that shows an animation of typing the question into Google and getting a real results page.[5] The sarcastic implication is that the person could have just as easily Googled the question themselves rather than asking you.)

Teaching your Social Customer Care employees about the most frequently asked questions will save you (and them) time later when they start to see these repetitive questions from prospects and customers. Many of these will be basic questions that require basic answers, such as:

- What are your store hours?
- What is the price of this product or service?
- How do I enroll in your program?
- How does your product or service work?
- Can I check on the status of my order?

Agents should be able to quickly answer each of these questions and/or direct a customer to the right place on your website to find the answer (this latter method can be helpful to others who scroll through your social feed because they may find the answer to the same question without even having to ask it).

There will also be frequently asked questions that are not basic but that are "known irritants." A known irritant is an issue that customers are having that the company is aware of but hasn't fixed yet. There may be several reasons for this, including:

- The project fixing the issue hasn't been prioritized, or is scheduled to be completed in several weeks or months
- A forthcoming product update will render the irritant obsolete
- The company has decided to accept the irritant as a cost of doing business

The irritant may also be "known" to the Customer Service department but not yet communicated to the business; this really shouldn't happen if you are following the suggestions in Chapter 10: Integrating With The Core Business. Regardless, make sure your agents understand how to respond to questions and complaints about the irritant, including potential work-arounds for the customer.

That said, it is important that your social media responses do not sound robotic, so give agents enough leeway to answer even repetitive questions in their own words.

"It's really important that we start with empathy and understanding so our team members are very much empowered to be who they are," said Telstra's Monty Hamilton. "There's no robotic scripts. There's no 'you must use these words and not those words'. Our people are real people and we empower them to have conversations in digital communities as they would with their friends and families in a physical environment."

Hamilton added that agents are taught to "learn, listen and understand what the frustration and challenge is [so] that we can try and improve and resolve for customers."[6]

INTERNAL SYSTEMS AND POLICIES

It's very important that all new employees understand the systems and software that will guide their day-to-day work, so take the time to thoroughly train them. It's a good idea to bring in a representative from your Social Customer Care technology provider to run the training. (The company may try to charge you for this but the fee can usually be negotiated. You might also consider adding this to your contract up front to account for future training needs.) Agents should thoroughly understand how to claim a post, tag it appropriately (usually with business or inquiry type classifications), answer the customer's questions, and close the inquiry.

New agents will also need to learn about complementary systems and software, which may include your CRM or account management system, Microsoft Office products, email and instant messaging software, and your company's intranet and Knowledge Base resources (containing FAQs, terms and conditions, and other useful information).

Don't forget to also train your agents on the digital properties that your customers use, like your website, Account Center, and mobile app. Encourage your agents to become actual customers, but if for some reason they can't, set them up with test accounts so they can actually log in and play around on the website and mobile app.

Most company policy training will be covered in a new employee's standard onboarding process, but you should ensure your Social Customer Care agents especially understand your company's Social Media Policy and any Social Customer Care policies or procedures that you have set up. (See Chapter 8 – Process.)

Similar to frequently asked questions, it is important to ensure that agents don't get overly bogged down in policies and procedures, creating hesitancy to respond in a personalized way.

Telstra's Hamilton simply tells his agents to "Be yourself."

"That's the number one message we give to all of our team members, every employee across the organization," he said. "Of course we have some policy and process, but that's very much focused on education and empowering people to do the right thing and helping them learn and understand what things might not be the right thing in different social networks, different communities. What works in Facebook doesn't always work in Twitter."[7]

SOCIAL MEDIA PLATFORMS

Take the time to walk through each social media platform that your company is using, explaining both the general mechanics of each one and the Customer Service-specific tools and processes. Don't assume that even seasoned social media experts know the ins and outs of all of the Customer Service functionality.

While the social media platforms are all competing for the same audiences, the reality is that they tend to serve different purposes in people's lives. For example:

- **Facebook** is often used most for interacting with family and friends, sharing stories and photos
- **Twitter** is often used most for obtaining real-time news and engaging with followers with whom you share a topical interest
- **LinkedIn** is often used most for professional networking and sharing of business-related content
- **Instagram** is for sharing visuals, both photos and videos
- **Pinterest** is for cataloguing interests using images
- **Snapchat** is for personal messaging and live video stories
- **Periscope** is for live-streaming longer content video

- **YouTube** has historically been most often used for pre-recorded video, but live video and social functionality have been added
- Messaging sites such as **Facebook Messenger**, **WhatsApp**, **WeChat**, and **QQ Mobile** are generally more private vehicles for messaging by text, images, and sometimes video

The difference between all these platforms, including their nomenclature (posts vs. tweets vs. pins, friends vs. followers, etc.), is critical to understanding consumers' expectations of your brand in each platform. Your Social Customer Care agents need to be fluent in each channel's functionality, audience type, etiquette and eccentricities (the most obvious one being Twitter's 140-character limit) that will affect how Customer Service is performed.

"We provide social media training and social media etiquette training," said Kriti Kapoor, former global director of Social Customer Care at HP Inc. "They need to understand the do's and do not's."[8]

It's important to note that social media platform training doesn't end at a new employee's orientation. Social media is notorious for changing on almost a daily basis (thus the reason I maintain there is no such thing as a true social media "expert") and your front-line agents need to be up-to-speed on new features and functionality. Twitter and Facebook especially have been pouring money into Customer Service delivery, each with the goal of making their channel *the* place for Customer Service for both consumers and companies. Consider that in just 12 months during 2015-16:

- **Twitter** introduced the *Customer Service on Twitter* Playbook with best practices and case studies; extended the character length of direct messages to 10,000 characters; published proprietary research linking Customer Service responses on Twitter to increased revenue; added coding that creates a link to a direct message rather than the customer having to go to a different place to initiate a DM; and added customer satisfaction surveys after the completion of a Customer Service engagement

- **Facebook** began allowing consumers to send messages to brands even if they don't follow them; introduced APIs that allow retailers to connect online orders to a Facebook Messenger account for automated updates; created "Messenger Bots" to leverage artificial intelligence (AI) to answer standard Customer Service questions; and worked with Sprout Social to create "Suggested Responses" based on previous similar questions

There is so much news at these companies, it's probably a good idea to hold monthly sessions with your Customer Service agents to ensure they know about the latest technology and functionality.

If all this sounds like a lot, it's because it is.

"We have a two-month training program," said Michelle Mattson of T-Mobile. "You're learning about the 'Un-carrier'. You're learning our internal systems. We're not going to put you out there in a public-facing environment without setting you up for success. It's a Herculean effort."[9]

Given that T-Mobile is best-in-class at Social Customer Care, ask yourself: Are you expending a "Herculean effort" to train *your* Social Customer Care agents?

COMMUNITY MANAGEMENT

In the last chapter, we talked about the different perspectives of the Marketing and Customer Service departments. Often, one area of contention is which group performs the role of "community management." This refers to responding to positive posts about the brand, which are often perceived as more fun and enjoyable and therefore representative of a "Marketing" role rather than a Customer Service one.

"So Marketing owns outbound messaging and maybe engagement like, 'Hey, I love you! I love you too!' messaging where then Care starts owning the actual responding to customers when you have real issues," said Sparkcentral's Kestens of how most companies initially divide up the work.[10]

In my experience, allowing Customer Service agents to also act as community managers is a win-win for everyone. Here's why:

- Customer Service agents are used to dealing with angry or upset customers all day long. This is hard work! It also can be soul-crushing, which can affect an agent's performance. Allowing them to respond to happy customers gives them a fun break from the naysayers and makes them more effective at handling the difficult posts.
- Customer Service agents are already trained on how to talk with customers, which is often not the case with marketers who don't regularly interact directly with customers.
- They are also trained on the software platform to respond to customers in social media, and are connected to the company's CRM to record conversations.
- It allows the Marketing department to focus on what it does best, which is crafting messages and experiences aimed at larger groups of consumers.

"We can recommend a successful model," the Sparkcentral *7 Steps* white paper proclaims. "Let your marketers 'push out' content… and let your CS agents take on everything that's inbound."[11]

PUBLIC CUSTOMER SERVICE

The last thing you need to ensure your agents understand is that performing Customer Service in public is much different that performing it on the phone. Traditional Customer Service agents are used to a one-to-one relationship with the customer; that is, the conversation is private between only two people. In social media, that is clearly not the case because there is always an audience. In his book, *Hug Your Haters*, Jay Baer refers to social Customer Service as "a spectator sport."[12]

So while it is important that the agent still tries to establish a one-to-one relationship with the customer – personalizing the conversation with the customer's first name and leveraging available customer information from social media profiles or the company's CRM – the agent must also think about what others will perceive about the conversation. Remember that even if you reply directly to a tweet, starting with the customer's handle, the response can still be seen by anyone and it can also appear in search results.

People who are not even part of the original conversation may decide to participate, either by adding their Likes and comments or by sharing a post with their audience, thereby exposing the conversation to even more people. Agents must thoroughly understand that everything they post is public, on behalf of the brand, and can be shared with a wider audience. A good rule of thumb is to ask of every post whether the company would be OK with it appearing on the corporate website. If yes, then the post is fine. If there are concerns, then you should look to re-write the post.

Most sophisticated technology platforms will allow you to classify a new employee in some sort of "approval" status, whereby each response he or she writes needs to be approved by a manager before it is actually posted. This is a good short-term strategy for getting new agents comfortable with responding publicly.

Public Customer Service can be fun and rewarding, especially when the company is customer obsessed and it already has a lot of fans. Customers love hearing from brands on social media – it makes them feel important and loved, and they will often share those good feelings with their friends and followers. But public Customer Service can also cause reputational risk to a company if it's not done correctly – if agents aren't properly trained or if posts aren't properly monitored. If you've trained your agents well, you can enter the world's most public Customer Service channel with confidence that you are helping to improve customer experience and brand reputation.

PROCESS
(WINNING AT SOCIAL CUSTOMER CARE STEP #5)

In some ways, the Process step is what brings everything together. The steps that you outline as part of your Process will serve as a roadmap to new and existing employees, as well as managers, leadership, auditors, regulators, and anyone else interested in your social Customer Service program.

Process also helps provide a consistently high level of Customer Service, which is key to retaining customers.

"Inconsistent service erodes confidence," said Shep Hyken. "And it doesn't even have to be inconsistent with bad service. It just has to be inconsistent."[1]

WHAT IS IT?

Your Process includes the steps which enable you to deliver superior Customer Service and business results, using your Philosophy, technology provider and people. It should include scenario planning for a wide variety of situations so your agents are well prepared for anything. That said, it can't be a 90-page manual that no one will read.

"Your process should be enough to stay safe but not too much to slow you down," said Dan Moriarty, formerly of Hyatt Hotels and now at the Chicago Bulls.[2]

Rob Hahn of Southwest Airlines describes his company's Process as akin to a "recipe":

"We're building more of a recipe of how we engage with our customers, how we speak to our customers," he said. "You're welcoming the customer, finding out what their problem is, researching their problem, and then giving them a resolution. So we walk through all those steps.

"With Customer Service, you could be interacting with somebody that just lost a loved one or they missed a certain special event because their flight was delayed. So we look at also the tone and how we should be approaching those different situations on a case-by-case basis."[3]

Let's look at some of the things you should consider including as part of your formal Process.

WHEN TO TAKE DISCUSSIONS OFF-CHANNEL

The decision to move a conversation off-channel may seem simple, but in reality there are a variety of factors and many situations are unique. It is always best to answer the question on the channel of the customer's choice if possible. Why? Two main reasons:

1) The customer likely knows you have other Customer Service channels, but has independently chosen to use social media instead. This may be because another channel has failed him/her, or it may be because social media is their first-choice channel. Serving the customer in the channel of their choice is the best way to ensure their happiness and satisfaction, and the last thing someone who's been on hold for two hours wants to hear is, "Please call our 800 number for assistance"!

2) Others in the social media community will be able to see that your company is responsive, that it cares for its customers, and that it provides great service. Your answer may also provide content to help others who have not even asked a question yet, potentially reducing future Customer Service expenses.

Moving a discussion off-channel or even offline still demonstrates responsiveness, but it runs the risk of looking like your company is hiding something, that it would prefer to sweep the question or complaint under the carpet than acknowledge and answer it publicly. And moving *every* question offline looks downright evasive and robotic.

"Redirecting customers away from their chosen support channel is one of the worst Customer Service experiences possible," says Conversocial's *Definitive Guide.*[4]

Still, asking a customer to move to Direct Message on Twitter or Facebook Messenger rather than a public page in order to provide personal information (to verify an account, for example) is a perfectly reasonable request. It may also be necessary in order to hear and understand the customer's whole story, the context of which may be lost in just 140 characters.

"It's not always possible for us to resolve those inquiries in a public digital channel so it's about having the right backup and support to take a private conversation that requires a certain security around identification into a live chat channel," said Monty Hamilton of Australian telecom Telstra. "We have a live chat service that's connected to our Facebook page where an inquiry is posted on Facebook and we need to complete an identification check with customers for security and privacy, we can take that inquiry into a one-to-one live chat session securely and have that dialogue with the customer in a private setting."[5]

Telstra's approach results in a great customer experience, and is very similar to the process I have used. The live chat session opens right within the Facebook (or Twitter) window, so it doesn't feel to the customer like he or she is "leaving" the channel. This solution likely becomes obsolete for companies that are comfortable using Facebook Messenger or Twitter Direct Message for these types of inquiries, but many companies do not trust the security of any other company but their own. Both Facebook and Twitter have made strides in improving the security of their direct messaging platforms with various encryption methods, but they will likely need to do more in the future to completely satisfy the Risk and Security teams at financial service and other regulated industry companies.

Generally, I'd suggest resisting the urge to move the discussion completely offline, like to telephone or email, for the two reasons listed above. But "offline" means different things to different people.

"When I say 'offline' I really just mean direct message or private message," said Michelle Mattson of T-Mobile. "We learned in 2014 that taking people really offline and into email is a no-no."[6]

That said, you have to know your own customers. What may be a "no-no" for one company's customers could be a "yes-yes" for another company's customers.

"We can't resolve everything end to end on social, so there's definitely still a need for our chat, voice, [and] email," said Allison Leahy, director of community at Fitbit. "A lot of customers do prefer email; it's our highest volume [channel]."[7]

Clearly, though, there are situations which absolutely require moving a conversation out of the public spotlight. Inquiries (or their answers) that include Personally Identifiable Information (PII) or Protected Health Information (PHI) must be taken to a private space immediately due to privacy laws.

PII is any information that can be used to identify a specific individual and is often separated into "sensitive" and "non-sensitive" information. You should check with your company's lawyers for their exact definition of sensitive PII, but examples include:

- Social Security Number
- Driver's License Number
- Birthdate
- Home address
- Personal telephone numbers
- Personal email addresses
- Mother's maiden name
- Account numbers
- Specific information related to marital status, children, financial accounts or transactions, employment or educational history, military records, or arrest records[8]

Non-sensitive information is that which is releasable to the public, such as information on one's business card. Where it gets tricky is when the customer includes sensitive PII in his or her social media post; while they are making their own sensitive information public, that doesn't necessarily give your company the right to verify or repeat it. Transactional information, such as an order number or a record locator, may be considered non-sensitive unless it is possible for someone to use that number to identify the customer. Again, check with your company's lawyers for exact details.

PHI is any information about health status, health care, medical conditions, medical records, and payment history that can be linked back to a specific individual.[9] There are usually tighter regulations on this kind of data due to the Health Insurance Portability and Accountability Act of 1996, or HIPAA, which prohibits use of PHI without the patient's written permission.

Since consumers may not understand privacy laws or even that it's not advisable to share personal financial or health information on social media, companies are expected to protect their customers' data no matter what. If you work in Social Customer Care long enough, at least one of your customers will share something that surprises you. When I worked at Discover, there were several occasions when customers (usually of Millennial age) posted pictures of their brand-new credit cards – including the full number! – for the world to see. Of course, the immediate advice back to the customer was to delete the post.

No matter which channel you end up using to service your customer, it is important that they receive the same response, if at all possible, in each channel. Some companies have created looser guidelines for Social Customer Care agents because the servicing is happening in public ("Just give them what they want so they'll stop complaining!") but this is a very slippery slope because customers may learn that social is the channel where a "no" answer can become a "yes." Remember what Shep Hyken said earlier about inconsistent service?

ESCALATION PROCEDURES

There are several scenarios in which you may need to escalate an issue that arises in social media, and your Process document should indicate who should be called and under which circumstances. The list below is not meant to be exhaustive, but it should give you an idea of the types of situations you should think about:

When to call management: Be sure to escalate issues where you think (or know) your company has really screwed up. This could be a faulty product, an erroneous marketing campaign, a system outage, or a particular circumstance where a customer was just not treated in the right way. These are generally issues that you won't be able to solve for the customer by yourself.

When to call Public Relations (PR): All inquiries from the media should immediately be sent to the PR (sometimes called Corporate Communications) department unless there is an official company spokesperson on the Social Customer Care team, which is rare. Any questions relating to your company's stock, earnings reports, or other investor/analyst questions should also be sent to PR and/or your company's Investor Relations department. In addition, any scenario that has the potential to devolve into a scandal or crisis should be immediately directed to PR so they can prepare an official company response that includes social media.

When to call Human Resources (HR): If you encounter an issue that involves any of your company's employees, it's time to engage the HR department. This can involve posts that reference specific employees (I once saw a soon-to-be-ex-wife lambasting an employee on the company's Facebook page), posts from disgruntled employees or ex-employees, any violations of your company's Social Media Policy, or general or specific threats against any employee. While the National Labor Relations Board (NLRB) has issued guidance detailing the circumstances under which employees can criticize their employer[10], each situation is unique and is best handled by HR.

When to call the police: If you ever encounter a post which discusses or threatens criminal activity or harm to oneself or others, you should contact local authorities. This is best done through your PR or Security department. It can sometimes be difficult to distinguish innuendo ("If they don't answer my call in the next 5 minutes I'm going to kill myself!") vs. an actual threat, but it's better to be safe. I had a case a few years ago of a woman with a seemingly legitimate complaint who, after posting several times about her depression and threatening in great detail to kill herself, received a visit from the police department at her home based on a call from our company. Even if you're wrong, you can rest easier knowing that you showed compassion and tried to do the right thing for another human being.

WHAT TO DO IN A CRISIS

The most important things to do in a crisis situation are to remain calm and have a plan. Oftentimes executives will get worked up about a small spike in mentions, or a story that seems like it could go "viral" but really isn't. Full-blown social media crises are actually pretty rare.

Having a plan means detailing procedures in your Process document so that anyone who is working Social Customer Care that day can easily begin implementing the agreed-upon steps. One of the first steps will likely be escalating the situation to one or more of the parties identified above.

One of the best examples that I have seen of escalation and response in a crisis situation came from United Airlines in July of 2015, when its computer systems were unexpectedly down for an extended period of time. I wrote a blog post[11] about the situation at the time, and am including the post here because it remains relevant. As you read it, think about the various Process pieces that United had to have in place in order to respond so quickly and seamlessly.

For anyone who works in social media, it's the biggest nightmare imaginable: computer systems are down, service is disrupted, and customers are angry. That's exactly what happened to United Airlines on July 8, [2015] when a "router issue" affected "network connectivity," according to a company statement.

Not surprisingly, United was deluged with posts on Twitter and Facebook, both from media mentions and – more often – from customers.

According to data obtained from Topsy.com, United saw an average of 1,736 daily mentions on Twitter in the 29 days before July 8, with a low of 802 on

July 3 and a high of 3,446 on June 8. On July 8, there were more than 14,300 mentions – or more than 8 times the daily average.

So how did United's social media team handle the increased volume? Amazingly well.

First of all, it appears that the company ceased all outgoing marketing in social media. This is important because pre-planned social media posts can appear out of sync or even insensitive during a crisis.

Next, at 7:43 AM Eastern, the airline proactively posted a tweet noting that "We experienced a network connectivity issue. We are working to resolve and apologize for any inconvenience."[12]

Many brands skip this crucial step of informing their customers of a problem. Usually the reasoning is "we don't want the whole world to know we're having a problem, so we'll just deal with the customers who complain." But this reasoning is faulty because what people want during a problem scenario is information, and if the brand doesn't provide information, it is liable to receive even more social media complaints. United did a great job of quickly owning up to the fact that there was indeed an issue, assuring customers that the airline was working to solve it, and apologizing for the inconvenience. Still think you can't say a lot in 140 characters?

At 8:33 AM, the airline posted an update on Twitter: "We're recovering from a network connectivity issue & restoring flight ops. We'll have a waiver on united.com to change flights."[13] Again, in a single tweet the airline did an excellent job of proactively alerting customers that the issue had been resolved, that flights would begin taking off again, and that change fee waivers were available on the website. The words "recovering" and "restoring" seem comforting, and the fact that a solution was offered in the form of a waiver likely answered a lot of passengers' questions. It should also be noted that both tweets received hundreds of retweets and favorites.

But United wasn't done. After the situation was resolved, the airline posted an apology on both Facebook and Twitter that read: "We know how important your travel plans are to you, and we're sorry for today's disruptions."[14] The posts were accompanied by a 42-second video of Sandra Pineau-Boddison, United's senior vice president for customers, who demonstrated empathy, transparency, and helpfulness. She humbly apologized – not once but twice – and offered solutions to passengers who still needed to get to their final destination. This is the epitome of great Customer Service.

Not surprisingly, it took United some time to respond to the massive influx of brand mentions on social media, just as it took some time to reschedule lots of flights. But well into the night, the airline was still responding individually to customers, even those who had tweeted hours earlier. These were no canned responses either; each one was unique, maintaining United's friendly tone and offering to help.

The reality is that mistakes will happen with every company. Technology will fail us. Human errors will occur. Products won't always operate as they were intended. And in today's world, customers may be quicker to complain publicly on social media, so brands have to be ready. It's clear that United had a detailed crisis plan in place that was extremely well executed at the critical moment.

Here is the full text of United's apology video:

"Hello my name is Sandra Pineau-Boddison and I'm Senior Vice President of Customers at United Airlines. First and foremost, let me apologize for the technology issues we had this morning. We absolutely recognize this is a disruption to your travel, and we do appreciate your business and loyalty. We have thousands of co-workers across the system working hard to get back on track as we've resolved the issues. I encourage you if you're traveling in the next day or two to go to united.com, go to the app; we have waived fees to be able to give you options to continue your journey going forward. So again, thank you so much for your loyalty and your business; we're continuing to work hard to earn it. And again, [we] apologize for the inconvenience."[15]

––––––––

Honestly, if you are going to have a social media crisis, this is exactly the way to handle it – with humility and empathy. My favorite part was the video featuring a senior executive; she conveyed a sincere desire to help the thousands of displaced passengers find their way to their original destination. Which executive in your company will be called upon to shoot a last-minute video in a time of crisis?

"As a company, own up," said Customer Service Consultant John R. DiJulius III in *The Customer Service Revolution*. "Don't make excuses about how or why it happened. Just come out and say it was handled incorrectly, and that you will make sure it is never handled that way again."[16]

United followed this recommendation perfectly.

EMPOWERING THE TEAM

Certainly your Process should include steps which allow your social Customer Service agents to resolve customers' problems, but it's even better to empower them to provide "surprise and delight" moments in special situations. A "surprise and delight" moment can really be anything unexpected for the customer; it should be genuine, show appreciation, and generally of nominal monetary value. Here are some great examples from brands that have appeared on the *Focus on Customer Service* podcast:

- **Spotify**, a streaming music service, answers some Customer Service inquiries with a personalized playlist (an excellent integration of its core product) that, when the song titles are read from beginning to end, spells out the answer to the customer's question.[17]
- **Vega**, a plant-based nutritional supplement company, often uses cartoons containing food puns, such as "That's quite the pickle," "Let's taco bout it" and "Kick some ass-paragus!"[18]

- **JetBlue**, a low-cost U.S. airline, once responded to a customer's request by calling his airport gate and getting Hulk Hogan's entrance music to be played when the customer entered the plane![19]
- **The Chicago Cubs** will proactively look for posts about celebrating birthdays at Wrigley Field and sometimes surprise a fan with a Cubs-themed gift right at their seat.[20]
- **Duke Energy** sends proactive social media communications in advance of big storms. "People in those situations feel like we're there for them, we're prepared," said Duke Energy's Madeleine Piercy. "I think it helps build confidence in our brand, that we are giving them the tools that they need to stay safe and be prepared."[21]

In addition, my former employer, **Discover**, used to select certain posts that were especially positive or helpful and send the customer a hand-written thank you note along with a gift card in the mail.

Notice that the first two examples above are a "surprise and delight" within the channel (social media), but the others take the experience offline. Both methods can be successful in driving customer loyalty to the brand. All of these brands also do a good job of integrating their core business or product into the experience; if Vega were to respond with music puns or if JetBlue were to play the customer's theme music when he walked into a coffee shop, it obviously wouldn't have the same effect.

Why is surprising and delighting customers important? As we discussed in the Customer Experience section, happy customers help your company in many ways. They tend to spend more with your company, have a longer tenure, are more resistant to competitors' temptations of sales and start-up promotions, have more patience when you mess up, and – perhaps most importantly – tell their friends about you, potentially bringing in even more happy customers.

Another benefit is that your Customer Service agents will be happier, too. It feels good to make someone's day, and happy employees lead to happy customers. So in the end, it's a win-win-win situation; the customer, the agent, and the company all benefit.

Amy Bivin of Dell said that "the key to your success is when you build your team, you want to make sure they're empowered to do anything."[22]

The Sparkcentral *7 Steps* white paper concurs, suggesting that agent empowerment is an absolute necessity: "If you don't empower your Customer Service agents with the authority and agency to resolve an issue, you've shot yourself in each foot before you even got out of bed."[23]

And Scott Wise of Scotty's Brewhouse said he has turned many detractors back into fans simply by going above and beyond to fix a problem: "If you've got a problem you take care of it five times over," he said. "You overcompensate because you can take somebody that's had the worst experience and turn them into the most raving fan by dealing with it the right way. You can also take a bad situation and make it worse by not taking care of it the right way."[24]

So how exactly do you empower your Social Customer Care agents? First, give them explicit permission to "make someone's day." Ashley Boone, the care social lead of women's online retailer ModCloth, said her agents often refer to themselves as "day makers" because their goal is to make every customer's day better.[25] They are trained to display empathy and to solve every customer's problem at (almost) any cost.

Next, you need to set some guidelines about what is and is not acceptable. Notice I used the word "guidelines"; that came from my two Customer Service expert friends, Shep Hyken and John DiJulius.

"I don't like the word 'rule' when it comes to Customer Service," said Hyken. "I like 'guidelines'. There's a line that you never want to cross and you try to teach anybody who's front-facing with the customer where that line is and that they can go all the way up to that line... And if I say yes and I've gone too far, my manager should use that as a teaching event and not something to berate me and make me feel bad about it."[26]

"Remove 'policy' from your employees' vocabulary," said DiJulius in *The Customer Service Revolution*. "This has become such a big issue, a crutch that reduces employees' Service Aptitude and causes them to sometimes make horrible decisions because they are afraid of going against 'company policy.'"[27]

In some regulated industries such as healthcare, there are very strict rules (with very strict penalties) about how much companies can spend on gifts for prospects or customers. The amount may be as low as $1 and is subject to auditing. Even if your industry is not regulated, you'll want to set a per-customer limit to ensure your agents don't go off the reservation and bankrupt the company. Alternatively, many brands give each agent a weekly or monthly budget with which to surprise and delight as many customers as they'd like. As long as they stay in that budget, everyone is happy.

Finally, try to create some reporting on the program. Getting to an explicit ROI [Return on Investment] will take time; it might take weeks or even months for a happy customer to recommend your brand to a friend, but it should happen eventually. In the interim, try measuring social media engagement metrics post-"surprise and delight" experience. Your customers will likely take to social media to thank you for your kindness.

RESPONDING TO COMPLIMENTS

Many brands don't bother responding to compliments on social media, which is a big mistake. The idea that somebody takes time out of their day to tweet at a brand or post on their Facebook page something positive about their experience is really incredible. Think about it: That never used to happen until social media became popular. A call center never got a lot of phone calls where the agent answered the phone and the person on the line said, "I'm just calling to tell you that you did a great job!" So take positive feedback for what it is – a gift – and be sure to respond to the person with a thank you.

"If you're only waiting until there's a problem to talk to your customers, then that's not indicative of a good relationship," said David Tull of Jack Threads.[28]

Customer Service expert Shep Hyken agrees. "If you get a positive comment, take advantage of having a short social conversation with that customer and letting them know how much you appreciate the opportunity. I think it's a mistake not to do it."[29]

Michelle Mattson of T-Mobile responds to all praise from customers, up to a point.

"We do have a lot of fan boys which is super cool and fan girls that will go back and forth in the 'we love you,' 'we love you too' and so my team has gotten really good at understanding where you can kind of draw the line and maybe just favorite a third or a fourth response and then kind of push it out [of the queue]," she said. "But where we don't stop is when customers really need an issue resolved. I think that's important because the majority of our volume is Customer Service and we have to be very diligent in going out and making sure we hit every issue, every time and then no one gets left behind."[30]

DEALING WITH TROLLS

Ah, trolls. Those nasty creatures that keep social media marketers and Customer Service agents up at night. A troll can be defined as a person looking for attention (in the form of an audience) through incessantly negative banter about a brand. This can often be confusing for Social Customer Care agents because they are used to people having problems that they try to solve. But trolls don't really want resolution; they want attention. Often their "complaint" is so amorphous that it isn't solvable anyway, and sometimes it has nothing to do with the company (in which case it also qualifies as spam).

The best way to deal with a troll is to respectfully answer the first post by offering to help. It's a good idea to offer to take the discussion offline so the person can rant privately instead of publicly. But here's the interesting part: Because trolls generally aren't looking for resolution, they are often surprised that the brand has engaged them at all. Many times, this will cause them to shut up. If, however, the person remains persistent after a couple of back-and-forths, it's OK to ignore and/or block the person from future communications.

"We handle this case by case," said Mattson. "We're good at touching every customer but if you're going to come at us with blazing middle fingers and like craziness that we just cannot reason with you on, we're not going to take the risk there."[31]

In Jay Baer's book, *Hug Your Haters*, he talks about the "Rule of Reply Only Twice," which implores companies to "Never, ever, ever, ever, EVER respond to someone more than twice."[32] In the case of trolls, this is a good rule to follow, as there is no benefit in continuing the dialogue. And Baer, like

Mattson, suggests that even with praise, there is a quickly diminishing return in answering multiple back-and-forth messages.

The tricky part comes when there is a real problem being addressed that may require more than two responses, and the customer seems willing to engage further. In that case, I recommend continuing the conversation until the customer is satisfied.

RESPONSE TIME

We talked earlier about the importance of response time, including the Jay Baer/Edison Research study which showed that brands aren't living up to customers' expectations, and the Twitter study which showed that customers are willing to pay more money to responsive brands. So it's critical that your Process outlines steps to ensure a quick response time.

What is a "good" response time? It depends on whom you ask and which social media platform you are managing. Response time expectations tend to be highest on Twitter because of its real-time nature. Even so, there is a wide range of response times – I've personally experienced American Airlines responding in 3 minutes, while a certain cable TV provider sometimes takes days or even weeks. On Facebook, there seems to be a little more latitude; most company executives I've interviewed have goals of less than an hour. Facebook assigns a tag to pages to indicate that they respond either "within minutes," "within an hour," "within hours" or "within a day."[33]

"You need to be within 30 minutes of answering someone, or you're a dinosaur," said iOgrapher Founder and CEO David Basulto.[34]

To achieve a fast response time, you'll need to lean on your Technology provider and your Training. As discussed earlier, some providers allow you to prioritize certain posts based on varying criteria, such as the influence of the poster or the urgency of the post. For example, Comcast might want to prioritize posts about a cable outage over posts asking what movies are playing on HBO this weekend.

Even if your Technology provider can't automate prioritization for you, it can still be done manually (depending on your volume of course). Either way, it is important to document your prioritization rules as part of your Process so it's clear to current and future agents and managers. You might want to start with these suggestions from Conversocial's *Definitive Guide*[35]:

First-tier priority:

- A customer asking the company a direct question
- A customer expressing dissatisfaction
- A customer that has an urgent product or service need
- Potential crisis issues

Second-tier priority

- General references to the company's products and services
- Positive experiences of the company's products and services
- Indirect references that are relevant to the company's industry

Training becomes integrated into Process as agents learn to use the technology and master the steps necessary to find, claim, respond to, and close an inquiry. Seasoned agents will usually have a series of shortcuts outlined on their computers, such as a list of responses to common questions and a list of contacts to call in case of a particularly complex inquiry. These shortcuts aid in reducing response time and should be shared with the rest of the team as appropriate.

If many of the inquiries you receive are complex, it may be necessary to respond quickly first just to let the customer know you are working on the issue, then respond again later when you actually have a resolution.

PLATFORM-SPECIFIC DECISIONS

There may also be platform-specific decisions that you need to make at this stage. For example, do you want to allow people to post directly on your brand's Facebook page? Most brands that are committed to social Customer Service allow this, because it makes it easier for people to share their opinions with your brand, but some companies are worried about wall posts interfering with marketing messages. This argument doesn't work, however, as organic reach has declined to almost zero and people can always share by responding to your marketing posts, which is usually less desirable.

"Typically what we see on Facebook is they're sharing their negative experience and commenting on our content because they know a lot of other people see that," said Dell's Amy Bivin. "And so the visibility is there and they're hoping that they can get help by posting [there]."[36]

On Twitter, the big question is whether to have a single brand handle or separate handles for marketing and Customer Service. Most people feel strongly about this decision, but not everyone agrees on the same answer, and some companies have even been changing their answer recently. As you'll see in a moment, I fall pretty squarely in one camp.

Most companies choose to have separate Marketing and Customer Service handles, both because it's easier for the company and because it separates Customer Service complaints from the string of marketing posts that the company so dearly wants us to see. The thinking is that service inquiries might cause the Marketing messages to get lost in the stream, or worse – someone might see that a customer has a complaint.

Making things easier for the company – instead of the customer – is a hallmark of old-school thinking, and that's inherently what's wrong with two separate Twitter handles in the first place. The expectation is that a customer desiring to contact a brand will spend the time to determine which handle is most appropriate before firing off that tweet. Of course, as most people who work in Social Customer Care know, this is not realistic, and the main handle ends up fielding many Customer Service inquiries anyway, sometimes awkwardly passing them to the appropriate service handle and many times not answering them at all.

In April 2016, after six years on Twitter, Delta Airlines decided to sunset its @DeltaAssist Twitter handle and combine it with the core @Delta handle.[37] Customer expectations, as well as technology advancements, made Delta's switch back to a single handle inevitable, though other companies have been slow to follow.

Customers don't have the time or the inclination to search for the appropriate handle when all they want is a speedy response and a resolution to their issue. And Delta uses a dedicated service provider (See Chapter 5: Technology) – software that was created exclusively for Social Customer Care and not publishing. Because of this, Delta can easily filter Customer Service inquiries from other forms of customer engagement, like responding to a marketing message or answering a poll question, rendering the separate handle unnecessary.

One other thing to consider is whether your company's CEO (or another executive) has an active presence on Twitter. If so, they are likely to receive Customer Service inquiries as well, so your Social Customer Care team should be ready to handle those as they come in. In this case, however, it is best practice for the personal account to respond and mention the Customer Service handle (along with a note like "my team will look into this for you"), which will then send the question to the Social Customer Care queue.

PROACTIVE CUSTOMER CARE

More and more sophisticated brands are learning that proactive customer care can create a great customer experience, provide marketing benefits like brand awareness, and even save Customer Service costs down the road. Proactive customer care can take several forms:

Indirect Mentions: This is when someone tweets or posts about your brand, but does not directly "tag" the brand with a handle. Look at the difference between these two hypothetical tweets:

@CoolBrand My new jeans ripped after wearing them only twice! What should I do?

Ugh, my new Cool Brand jeans ripped after wearing them only twice! What should I do?

If Cool Brand is practicing proactive customer care and using the proper technology to "listen" for brand mentions in social media, it shouldn't matter that the second tweet above didn't include their official handle. Cool Brand should be constantly "listening" for terms like "Cool Brand jeans" and jumping in to respond and help customers who may not even be asking the brand for help.

Proactive Alerts: This is when a company tells its customers that something is wrong before the customers have a chance to complain about it. A typical example is when a company's website or call center is down, it is helpful to send an outgoing message in social media to alert people before you receive an onslaught of incoming messages.

Duke Energy has found success with this tactic, especially in advance of a big storm. "We've seen really great results from doing that," said Madeleine Piercy. "People in those situations feel like we're there for them, we're prepared. I think it helps build confidence in our brand, that we are giving them the tools that they need to stay safe and be prepared."[38]

Industry Mentions: This is when brands use social listening to identify trends or pain points within their larger industry, rather than about the company itself. Perhaps people are experiencing a common problem with your industry that your company has recently solved. It may be useful to step in and suggest that you are there to help. T-Mobile being the first U.S. carrier to eliminate contracts is a great example; they could have listened for people complaining about long, expensive cell phone contracts and inserted themselves in the conversation with a better alternative.

Recognizing Milestones: This is when brands reach out to people to celebrate an event or an accomplishment. It could be someone's birthday, wedding, new job, pet adoption, or birth of a child; it could also be someone's first 5K race, someone deciding to go gluten free, or someone beating cancer. The key is to identify potential or current customers who are celebrating something and send a personalized message from your brand.

Competitor Mentions: Some brands have had success stepping in when someone is complaining about a competitor and suggesting that the person choose their company instead. Tread lightly here; not only can this feel a little "big brotherish" to consumers, but you may also be inviting your competitors to do the same for people who are complaining about your company. If you are going to try this, start small and measure results carefully to ensure that the reward is bigger than the risk.

Proactive customer care is not required, but if you do it, you should outline a Process for what's in and out of scope, just like you will have done for the other activities listed above.

There are many things to consider when developing a Process document, and you will probably not be able to address every conceivable scenario that your agents may face. While I've highlighted some key considerations in this chapter, there are many others that could be included, and your company may have unique situations which should be addressed. It is OK (and even encouraged) to make this a "living and breathing" document which is reviewed, updated, and shared with the Social Customer Care team regularly.

Speaking of sharing, one more best practice in Process is to review social responses with the team on a regular basis. Social media is fast-paced and ever-changing, and it's a huge benefit to take a step back and look at a random selection of posts and responses to ensure that your Process is being followed, your Training has worked, and your Philosophy remains intact. Try to use even poor responses as learning opportunities for agents rather than examples cited for punishment. Remember that Social Customer Care agents need a certain amount of leeway, and it is management's job to ensure they know where the guardrails are.

REPORTING
(WINNING AT SOCIAL CUSTOMER CARE STEP #6)

As with any corporate initiative, it is important to measure results and report progress up to management. But social media is notoriously difficult to measure because it doesn't always conform to "typical" marketing metrics. Social media teams have had to educate seasoned executives on metrics such as Likes, Follows, Comments, Shares, and Retweets, and also try to explain why these metrics matter. Add to that the fact that for many brands, social media plays at the very top of the marketing funnel (awareness), executives have been asked to "believe" – or as Jay Baer succinctly puts it, to "Embrace the Power of Eventually."[1]

Thankfully, the Key Performance Indicators (KPIs) for social Customer Service are likely more recognizable to executives, especially those involved in operations roles. Many of the metrics we will review here have comparable metrics in the call center world. The key is identifying which metrics your company cares about most, and then how you can easily obtain them each month. Most of the Technology providers we reviewed in Chapter 5 can provide the needed reporting, though there may be KPIs specific to your business that you'll either need to ask your provider to customize, or figure out a way to derive them yourself.

KEY PERFORMANCE INDICATORS

The following list should provide you with sufficient reporting to adequately understand how your social Customer Service program is performing. You may or may not need every one of these metrics, and there may be others specific to your business that can assist in telling your story to management.

Volume: One of the first things executives usually want to know about social media is what kind of volume the company is experiencing. This is tricky because the volume will likely not come close to that seen in other Customer Service channels. Still, every Customer Service post is public, so in some ways it is "worth" more than a single phone call or email.

"Even though the volumes are fairly low, there is still a thing to be said about the ROI in regards to saving money, preventing people to actually call in or use the more expensive communication channels within your contact center," said Sparkcentral's Davy Kestens. "For most of our customers, it's less than 2 percent of their entire communications within the contact center but that… is not necessarily a negative thing. I think companies are starting to realize that [social media] is a leading indicator of a much larger problem or a much larger opportunity that is happening within the entire customer care space."[2]

Reporting on volume also allows you to establish a baseline of what "normal" volume looks like and how high the "spikes" might be, identify seasonal or day-of-the-week trends to help with resource planning, and quantify the impact of acute events like a website outage or a public relations crisis.

Don't confuse Volume with the social media marketing metric of Mentions. The latter includes every time a brand is mentioned; here, we are talking about the posts that warrant a response from Customer Service. Sprout Social estimates that 56% of social messages that retailers received during the holiday season of 2016 required a response.[3] Your Technology provider can help with measuring this for your brand, using an algorithm that looks at identifiers such as question marks, @mentions and certain keywords.

Conversocial's *Definitive Guide* helps clarify why the distinction in the two metrics is meaningful: "You cannot control inbound volumes or your volumes by category. Rather, these metrics are important for providing a baseline from which to understand your other metrics. It's hard to understand what a change in handling or response time means unless you can match them up with changes in volume over social channels."[4]

Response Time (or First Response Time): This is the length of time between when a person first posts to your brand and when your brand first responds. It is important to note that the clock must start when the person posts because that is how the customer experiences the clock starting. Some companies make the mistake of starting the clock when they receive the post, which may be delayed by the Technology provider, a slow internet connection, or a post coming in during non-working hours. But that misses the point of reporting on how long the customer had to wait for an answer. If you want to be best in class for Response Time, aim for 15 minutes or less – even if that means responding first and resolving later.

"Response time is critical," said Michelle Mattson of T-Mobile, which is routinely best in class for Response Time. "I love to see when our customer surveys come back and they're like, 'Woo, I did not expect you to respond so quickly.'"[5]

Don't worry if your brand isn't there yet. The point of the Reporting is to monitor where you are so you can develop a Process over time that will improve the numbers. Plus, "best in class" is a continually moving target, as evidenced by Rob Hahn's "dream" for Southwest Airlines:

"I think everybody's dream would be less than a minute to get back to customers," he said. "So that's one thing we're doing is looking at how do we need to staff our team to get to those quick response times because that's where our customers are in the moment, dealing with the situation. They want that answer as soon as possible so that's definitely what we're working to is, as fast as possible."[6]

Note: It is not necessary to track multiple response times, so if you end up responding more than once, you can simply report on First Response Time.

It is OK to respond before you have a resolution; remember Twitter's data that showed this has a big effect on a customer's willingness to pay more to a company. "Even when an issue cannot be resolved immediately, it is important that an agent show the customer—and everyone who might see the post—that the company has heard the message and is working on a solution," says Conversocial's *Definitive Guide.*[7]

Resolution Time (or Handling Time): This is the length of time between when a person first posts to your brand and when your brand resolves the person's issue. Clearly if you resolve the issue in the first response, then Resolution Time will equal Response Time. But this is not always the case, either because there are several messages back and forth with the customer before a resolution is achieved, or because you need to take the customer offline via direct message or some other channel. Therefore, Resolution Time – or the difference between Response Time and Resolution Time – may be a good indicator of the complexity level of social media inquiries and/or your team's ability to quickly identify solutions.

"Handling Time covers all activity, including elements such as reading, tagging, marking sentiment, looking up customer account info, making notes and drafting responses," the Conversocial *Definitive Guide* explains. "Handling Time is one of the first truly cross-channel metrics for social Customer Service, enabling you to compare the performance of social against other channels. If it takes 10 minutes to resolve an issue via email and five minutes to resolve an issue on social, you have a solid justification for the ROI of your social Customer Service operation."[8]

Agent Performance: Everyone knows that averages can be misleading, which is why it is important to include agent-specific metrics in your Social Customer Care reporting. By looking at each agent's numbers – including Response Time, Resolution Time, Number of Inquiries Handled (usually per hour) and even Customer Satisfaction Scores (using, for instance, Twitter's customer feedback functionality) – you can get a better sense of what (or who) is impacting your overall performance numbers. At a past employer there was an agent who was consistently several minutes faster than all of the other agents at responding; once we identified her through our reporting, we were able to interview her for best practices that were then shared with the rest of the team. Likewise, agent-specific reporting will help you identify agents who are underperforming and may require additional training or supervision.

Team or Center Performance: Similarly, groups of agents may perform differently so if you are handling Social Customer Care out of multiple call centers, you should consider breaking out the reporting accordingly.

Performance variance may be due to a variety of factors, including team or center leadership commitment, the local agent talent pool, new hire training, business hours, or equipment.

Time-Based Performance: Measuring and reporting on results by hour, shift, or day will provide insight into volume trends, which can have a big impact on performance if you are not properly staffed. A daytime or evening shift should be relatively stable, but you should look for and try to explain any major shifts or outliers. An overnight shift might have more variance because the volume is likely to be significantly lower, often requiring agents to multi-task on another service channel. Time-based performance can also be used to indicate your brand's ideal servicing hours. While some multi-national brands may be required to have 24/7 coverage, your brand might be just fine with regular business hours or perhaps some extended hours to cover the majority of posts.

If you are not 24/7, you may want to report on business hours and non-business hours separately. On one hand, the late-night posts will skew your Response Time averages because they sat for a long time, so you may want to adjust for that lag. On the other hand, don't forget that an actual customer was indeed waiting that long for a response, so it is technically accurate.

Note that some outliers may be unpredictable (due to a crisis, weather, technology problem, product malfunction, etc.) but others may be due to lack of communication throughout the organization. For example, maybe the Marketing department decided to spend a lot of money promoting a certain social media post but forgot to tell the Customer Service team. Or maybe the Corporate Communications department put out a press release that is eliciting a lot of discussion on Twitter. Or maybe the Operations team sent out a letter sharing bad news to thousands of customers. Even someone from your company speaking at a conference may result in an abnormal spike in social media inquiries. This is why internal communication and collaboration is so critical.

Channel Performance: This is simply another cut of the data above, but separating out the individual social media channels. There are two reasons this is important. First, customer expectations can vary between channels. Twitter has always been known as a "real-time" platform that requires "real-time" responses. On Facebook, customers are a little more understanding – an hour may be fine for your business. Second, this is another way to untangle averages in the data which might be misleading. For example, a single response time number may not reflect the fact that your brand receives 75% of its inquiries on Facebook, where response time is more lenient. So your overall number might look high by Twitter standards, even if your actual response time on Twitter alone is much lower.

Sentiment: This refers to the overall emotion displayed in a post, and is usually distinguished as either Positive, Negative, or Neutral. This is the most complicated and misunderstood social metric because it can be extremely difficult to determine the actual sentiment of a particular post. Technology – even the best text analytics tools – cannot, to my knowledge, reliably differentiate sarcasm, slang, acronyms, abbreviations, foreign words, and other elements 100% of the time. So the best you can hope to achieve with this metric is a general sense for how well your brand is liked, and trending information to determine if sentiment is changing.

The key is to clearly define Positive, Negative, and Neutral for your company. For example, at one of my employers, a retweet of a brand tweet was considered Positive because one of the goals of Marketing tweets is to gain shares. At another employer, it was decided that a straight retweet should be considered Neutral because there was no additional commentary from the user. Neither answer is right or wrong as long as the definitions are applied consistently. It is important, however, that the data mean something and be actionable. If 98% of your posts end up Neutral because of your definitions, it's time to refine your definitions.

One other thing you may want to look at is Sentiment Conversion. This calculates the number (or percentage) of customers that the brand has successfully moved from detractor level (missed expectations) to advocate level (meets or exceeds expectations). This is a powerful indicator, and one that can be considered uniquely social media because it is really the only channel in which customers publicly share their experiences with others.

Post-Service Engagement: One of the most enlightening metrics – and the one that the Marketing department will care about most – is Post-Service Engagement. This is a measurement of traditional engagement metrics – Likes,

Comments, Shares, Retweets – after the Customer Service inquiry has been resolved. Start the clock after the brand posts what is believed to be the final response that resolves the customer's problem.

Unbelievably, I've found that engagement rates in both Facebook and Twitter after the service inquiry is resolved can be routinely over 100% – that is, at least one like, comment, share, or retweet of the final post *per customer*. Compare that to even the best of marketing campaigns, which likely see a single-digit engagement rate, and you begin to realize just how powerful Customer Service in social media can be. In fact, some have even dubbed it "one-to-one marketing."

Satisfaction Scores: As with any channel, you can measure customer satisfaction (or CSAT) scores in social media to get another indicator of how you are performing. In 2016, Twitter added the ability to insert a single customer satisfaction survey question at the end of a Direct Message Customer Service engagement. Sparkcentral reports its clients are seeing a 70+% completion rate on Twitter surveys.[9]

Likewise, Facebook has added capabilities in Messenger that allow for a quick post-engagement survey. Of course, you can always use external tools like SurveyMonkey, Foresee, or Opinion Lab which can provide links to insert in social media channels to collect data.

Whatever you choose, it is important to measure customer satisfaction on a regular basis. More than likely, you'll be able to draw a clear connection between your Response Time and Customer Satisfaction KPIs. You can also compare social media customer satisfaction scores to those of other service channels.

Cost Per Resolution: This is an advanced metric that usually takes companies a while longer to establish. That said, most traditional call centers are already measuring this for phone calls and maybe even email and chat. At nearly every company we've talked to for the *Focus on Customer Service* podcast, servicing customers on social media is cheaper than servicing them in other channels. But how do we calculate those costs? Unfortunately it's a bit complicated, and you will likely need some help and validation from your Finance department.

Here are the inputs you'll need:

1) The number of hourly or daily inquiries handled in social media
2) The average time it takes to resolve each inquiry
3) The average hourly rate paid to social media Customer Service agents
4) The standard overhead expense allocated to hourly workers in the call center (this accounts for fixed expenses like rent, utilities, and amortization of equipment)
5) The percentage of an agent's shift that is considered "down time"

To calculate the Cost Per Resolution in social media, add the average hourly rate of an agent and the standard hourly overhead expense, then multiply by the percentage of time allocated to social media Customer Service. If the agent is 100% dedicated to social media Customer Service, then simply multiply by 100%. But companies with lower volume levels may have agents that are not 100% dedicated to social media. If that's the case, make sure you track the agents' time allocated to social vs. other channels like phone or email so that you can paint an accurate picture of the real cost in each channel. (Overhead and other fixed costs should then be prorated across the channels based on the agents' allocations.) If an agent has "down time" during an hour, it should be allocated to each channel based on the percentage of time spent on that channel. For example:

Suzanne is a Customer Service agent who spends an average of 60% of each hour handling social media inquiries. When there are no inquiries to handle, she fills most of the remaining time (30% of her total) answering customer emails. Approximately 10% of her time is considered "downtime" – coffee breaks, team meetings, and other non-working activities. When calculating Suzanne's percentage of time allocated to social media Customer Service, we should start with the 60% and then add social media's portion of her downtime, which in this case would be 6% (60% of 10%), to get 66% total.

Next we divide the resulting number by the average number of social media customer resolutions in an hour. Note: the number of hourly customer resolutions need not be a whole number; that's why we collected the average resolution time. So if the average resolution time is, say, 25 minutes, then the average number of social media customer resolutions in an hour would be (60 min/25 min = 2.4 customers). This helps account for the fact that unlike telephone calls, social interactions can sometimes span hours or even days, due to waiting for the customer to respond. This makes it very difficult to measure "actual" time per discreet customer interaction.

So the mathematical equation of Cost Per Resolution will result in a dollar amount as follows:

$$\frac{(\textit{Avg. Agent Hourly Rate } + \textit{Standard Hourly Overhead Expense}) \times \textit{Social Media Time Allocation Percentage}}{\textit{Avg. Social Media Resolutions Per Hour}}$$

Once you have a Cost Per Resolution, compare it to other service channels. Those figures are likely readily available if your company has had a call center for a number of years; you just have to ask for it. In most large companies it's a fairly straightforward calculation because call center agents are consistently busy during the day – in other words, there is very little down time which needs to be accounted for, and most agents are not splitting their time across service channels.

What does your cost comparison look like? Twitter reported in its *Customer Service on Twitter* Playbook that service on Twitter could cost as little as 1/6 of a Customer Service phone call[10], though most comparisons I've seen are closer to 1/3. Either way, it is significantly cheaper, which emphasizes the importance of reporting its cost. Though volumes are comparatively low today, as they rise the cost benefit will quickly multiply. And remember: It is almost always less expensive to keep a customer than it is to obtain a new one, and social Customer Service undoubtedly helps companies keep more customers.

These calculations also assume that every social media inquiry would have otherwise resulted in a phone call, which we know is not likely true. (Millennials are well-known for avoiding phone calls at almost any cost, for example, so a better assumption would be that some but not all social media inquiries replace phone calls, while the rest are incremental.) In addition, it may exclude interactions that are better classified as "community management" than Customer Service. So it may be appropriate for your business to also calculate Cost Per Interaction, whereby the denominator in the above equation is Avg. Social Media Interactions Per Hour. This can be a useful metric to help determine the operational efficiency of the Social Customer Care team, but it is not an apples-to-apples comparison of phone call costs because there is no real equivalent to "community management" on the phone.

Again, you'll want your Finance department to verify all of your assumptions and calculations so you can use the result to hopefully request more resources for the Social Customer Care Team!

Top Issues: It is very important that you capture and report on the feedback that you are receiving in social media. Without doing so, your company won't be able to fix any of the issues that are raised by prospects and customers. We'll talk more about this in Chapter 10: Integration with the Core Business.

Competitive Analysis: It always helps to compare your results to others in your industry so you have a benchmark to determine whether you are doing well or not. Sprout Social analyzed data compiled from 236,000 public social profiles on Facebook, Twitter, and Instagram and more than 3.6 billion messages sent and received during a one-year time period during 2015 and 2016. They looked at Average Response Rate (percentage of eligible posts responded to), Average Response Time, Average Percentage of Messages Needing a Response, and Average Posts Per Replies (how many promotional messages brands publish compared to how many responses they give their audience). They then assigned a Brand Engagement Ranking (based on how responsive brands are to customers) and a Consumer Engagement Ranking (based on how vocal customers are with brands) across 15 industries. Their results are below[11]:

Brand & Consumer Index Spotlight by Industry

Q3 2016

Industry	Avg. Response Rate	Avg. Response Time (Hours)	Avg. % Messages Needing Response	Avg. Posts per Replies	Brand Engagement Ranking	Consumer Engagement Ranking
Automotive	10%	12.6	42%	19.9	#13	#13
Banking/Finance	12%	10.3	42%	26.9	#4	#9
Consumer Services	13%	14.3	39%	16.9	#9	#6
Education	8%	9.0	36%	22.1	#11	#11
Government	9%	10.4	40%	17.7	#12	#5
Healthcare	8%	10.5	44%	21.0	#15	#4
Internet/Technology	12%	11.3	36%	22.3	#5	#10
Marketing/Advertising	11%	12.4	38%	18.8	#10	#16
Media/Entertainment	7%	9.2	38%	111.2	#16	#15
Nonprofit	8%	10.0	38%	19.3	#14	#7
Professional Services	9%	8.9	32%	27.6	#7	#14
Real Estate	11%	11.0	47%	21.5	#6	#1
Retail	16%	11.5	46%	18.1	#3	#8
Travel/Hospitality	15%	10.1	46%	13.9	#2	#3
Utilities	17%	8.6	38%	16.4	#1	#2

sproutsocial

sproutsocial.com/index

Notice that Response Rates overall are low, likely due to there being a lot of "noise" in social media (again, the difference between Mentions and Customer Service Volume). Average response time is, on the whole, way above what is considered to be "best in class." Utilities, Travel/Hospitality, and Real Estate are the best performing industries and are thus the ones brands should be looking to emulate in social media.

Although this may seem like a lot of information, once you set up your reporting it should be relatively simple to maintain. Your Technology provider should be able to capture most of this data, and much of the reporting can be automated. Make sure you review the results with management periodically rather than just sending the report via email so you can get credit for your outstanding work!

10

INTEGRATION WITH THE CORE BUSINESS (WINNING AT SOCIAL CUSTOMER CARE STEP #7)

Now that you've established your Social Customer Service Philosophy, chosen the appropriate Technology Provider, hired a skilled staff and trained them thoroughly, established and documented a Process, and created meaningful Reporting for management, your Social Customer Care program is likely running quite well. You may be asking yourself, "Is this it? Have I arrived? Have I already conquered this complex and ever-changing world of Customer Service in social media?"

Well, you are certainly off to a strong start and are likely performing better than many other brands out there. But there's always opportunity to do more, and this chapter will teach you how to become more sophisticated in your handling of social media as it relates to other areas of your business. It is definitely more advanced than some of the earlier steps, but it is critical to maintaining a strong product or service and a tight relationship with your customers. This is where we connect back to the Customer Experience learnings at the beginning of the book.

We call this part "Integration with the Core Business."

WHAT IS IT?

Integration with the Core Business means that the Social Customer Care team is engaged with other business units to ensure that customer complaints are heard and customer ideas are shared. It's the second half of the "continuous cycle" described earlier, whereby offline experiences are shared online, and then a brand's response – and the learnings it takes from customer interactions – are incorporated back into the offline experience.

There are two ways in which Integration with the Core Business can provide value to your company:

1) Customer feedback, sometimes called Voice of the Customer, can help to improve existing products, services, and experiences
2) Customer ideas and use cases can help the Product Development team develop new products or services.

VOICE OF THE CUSTOMER

We already know that customers are not shy about sharing their opinions in social media. The big question is, what do companies do with the feedback? Responding quickly and resolving problems are essential steps, but they generally only treat the symptoms. Reporting is important to demonstrate operational efficiency and success, but we can't be guaranteed that the right people are reading it. In order to actually solve recurring customer issues, companies need to dig deeper to find the underlying causes and fix them. Only then will the complaints diminish. Luckily, social media is a great platform to help accomplish this.

When things go wrong, companies will hear about it on social media – early and often. And although we love engaging with our customers, if the Social Customer Care team sits within a Customer Service or Operations group, it is likely going to be held to certain cost standards that will limit the extent to which increasing service inquiries is possible. Zappos has said publicly that they "embrace long phone calls"[1] – and famously held an 10-hour, 43-minute extravaganza with one customer[2] – but most companies are trying to reduce Customer Service expense. While it is certainly debatable whether this is a good goal or not – Jay Baer laments that companies spend $500 billion per year on marketing but only $9 billion on Customer Service[3] – cost controls are just a reality of call centers today.

One way that the Social Customer Care team can control costs – and begin to demonstrate solid ROI to management – is to not only resolve Customer

Service complaints, but to help fix underlying problems and prevent future complaints from occurring. This requires Social Customer Care agents (and management) to have a solid understanding of how the rest of the business works, and which leaders can affect change.

For example, a credit card company might see regular complaints about certain transactions not qualifying for a bonus in the rewards program. Rather than just recording the complaint as "Rewards – Transaction Didn't Qualify," if the Social Customer Care Team can record the name of the affected merchant, they may be able to identify a pattern and alert the Merchant Relations team to fix the problem. Maybe a gas station at a warehouse club is showing up as a Discount Store purchase rather than a Gas or Fuel purchase on customers' statements, so it's not earning the associated bonus points for spending at gas stations. This is a relatively simple fix but it can't be done by the Customer Service department.

If the Social Customer Care Team recognizes that the same question keeps popping up about the same merchant, they can play a lead role in getting the problem fixed, thereby reducing complaints in the future.

Why is the Social Media Team better equipped than some other Customer Service teams to do this? Because virtually all of their interactions are in text form, so they can be captured, searched, and analyzed more easily than say, telephone calls. In fact, simple word cloud software may expose keywords that identify problems.

The key to success is ensuring that the Voice of the Customer is heard by other parts of the organization, so make sure to establish relationships with key leaders in each major area of the company so that you can meet regularly and share what you are hearing in social media about their part of the business.

FEEDBACK LOOP

One of the biggest benefits of social listening is the feedback you get from prospects and customers about your product or service. But that benefit is completely wasted if you don't do anything with this critical information. Feedback is a gift – in life and in business. Even negative feedback is extremely valuable because it allows companies to see clearly what's working and what's not working about their product, service, employees, or really any part of the customer experience.

"I respond to every single guest whether it's positive or constructive. And I either thank them and let them know that I'm going to thank their server or bartender or whomever gave them a good experience, or if it's constructive, I also thank them for the feedback. I let them know that I appreciate it," said Scott Wise of Scotty's Brewhouse. "And I found that that one thing that we do in my opinion makes us more successful than almost anything else that we do in this restaurant: The fact that we listen to people on a daily basis and we respond and we act."[4]

Let's look briefly at three kinds of feedback that you may see:

Compliments: When someone takes the time out of their day to compliment your company, it's clearly a nice gesture, but it also gives you valuable feedback about what your company is doing right. Your response (besides thanking the customer!) should be to figure out how to do more of that so you can make more customers happy.

Questions: When someone asks your brand a question, it's usually because they're genuinely interested. But if one customer has a question, chances are that others have the same question, so your takeaway is to figure out what part of your process or experience is causing that question and try to get it fixed. It may just be that one of your communication channels isn't clear to customers.

One other way to integrate with the core business is to use social media listening for content marketing ideas. Just as Google search queries can identify what questions prospects and customers have about your company or industry, so too can social media inquiries. By tracking and reporting on frequently asked questions, you can provide your Marketing counterparts with ideas for new content to appear on your company's website, mobile app, or social media properties. If someone asks your brand a question on social media, chances are more people have the same question. If those people are able to self-serve and find the information themselves, then that's fewer social Customer Service inquiries, which helps to reduce operational costs.

Complaints: Don't be afraid of complaints! Many executives don't want to be in social media at all because they are afraid of the bad things people will say about the brand. Well guess what? They're saying them anyway, so you might as well be part of the conversation.

As Jay Baer explains in his terrific book, *Hug Your Haters*, "Complainers aren't your problem; ignoring them is." In fact, he said, complainers are "the canary in the coal mine" – that is, they are often the first sign of trouble. His advice? "Answer every complaint, in every channel, every time."

"The customer is not always right," he adds, "but the customer always deserves to be heard."[5]

Baer's book describes two kinds of "haters": Offstage haters use traditional Customer Service channels such as phone and email, and usually desire a resolution to their problem. Onstage haters, on the other hand, use public channels such as social media, forums, and review sites, and usually desire a sympathetic audience more than a resolution. When you fail Offstage haters, you create Onstage haters.[6]

Listen to complainers, try to solve their individual problem, then look for the underlying issue – usually a process improvement – that will prevent the problem from recurring. Fitbit has installed this as part of its Process, with Allison Leahy saying her Social Customer Care team aims to "organize information around emerging issues and to troubleshoot and gather information from customers who may be experiencing a certain type of issue… bring[ing] that back to our engineering teams."[7]

Remember, when customers are reaching out with suggestions on how to improve your product or service, generally it means that they really care and that they're brand loyal.

"A complaining client is giving us the opportunity to make things right," said John R. DiJulius III in *The Customer Service Revolution*. "It's the silent ones that hurt us. They don't remain silent once they leave our business."[8]

By listening, responding, and resolving, your customer experience will improve dramatically over time as customer irritants are removed.

"We're human beings in a human world and we're going to make mistakes and not every guest is going to listen to you and be okay with that," said Scott Wise.

"But nine out of 10 are going to say, 'I appreciate the fact that you just owned up to it. I appreciate that you apologized to me. I'll be back in your restaurant next week and give you another try because you clearly care about Customer Service.'"[9]

Suggestions: Many companies have used social listening to collect new product ideas from customers. Similar to complaints, it's important that you know the right people in your organization who can properly evaluate and act on new ideas. Three companies that I interviewed for the *Focus on Customer Service* podcast shared great success stories using this strategy:

OtterBox: When OtterBox started noticing an uptick in complaints related to phones getting wet (and customers blaming the case), the team dug a little deeper into the social media posts and found something surprising: Customers were taking their phones into the shower with them to listen to music! Although OtterBox's original products were not designed to be used in the shower, this customer behavior – recognized by the Social Customer Care Team and communicated to the Product Development Team – resulted in the product launch of a brand-new waterproof case.[10]

Vega: This plant-based natural supplement company noticed that customers either loved or hated the taste of their products. But rather than continually responding to the haters with empty apologies, Vega started creating and sharing smoothie recipes that helped improve the taste of several of its nutritional powders. The result? Customers learned a new way to use the product, and Vega effectively prevented many customers from looking for alternative products.[11]

Fitbit: The fitness wearables company recently added a "Reminders to Move" feature, a buzzing reminder on the Fitbit device that encourages the user to get up and take some steps. Users in Fitbit's community forums came up with the idea and had self-titled it "Idle Alert," but the core idea was the same. The company also added new clock faces to its devices based on customer feedback and requests. "Fitbit is trying to be everywhere you are and more so a lot of what we do here is look at how we can expand our services and listen more broadly, and most importantly incorporate all of our great customer feedback into the products and services we develop," said Allison Leahy.[12]

Find the right parties within your larger organization who have the ability to improve your product, service, and/or customer experience. Reporting on customer feedback is not enough; you need to make sure the reporting gets to the right people and that they take action on it. Leahy said her team sends "qualitative and quantitative reporting out to those product and feature teams on a weekly basis, [and] if the Engineering team has more questions about what the users really expect to see or want to see then we can start engaging in that conversation."[13]

Shep Hyken agrees: "I've always felt that in every negative situation, you can't just fix the problem. You've got to restore confidence," he said.[14]

That said, it may not be practical to fix every issue that emerges in social media. When you create customer feedback reporting, be sure to include volumes so management can distinguish between recurring problems that need to be addressed, and one-off issues that may be anomalies or due to "user error."

Finally, notice that I referred to a feedback *loop*. That's because if done correctly, the process should come full circle to a conclusion. The customer provides feedback, you respond by thanking the customer and sharing the feedback with the proper department, they act on the feedback, and you "loop" back to let the customer know that their feedback had an impact.

Of course, change takes time at most companies, so the final "loop" won't happen immediately. But one of the easiest and best ways to impress your customers and create brand advocacy is to circle back to them when your company has made changes based on their suggestions. This could range from a minor product improvement to the elimination of a customer irritant to the creation of a brand-new product. Whether the change occurs days, weeks, or even months later, try responding (again) to the original post(s) to let your customers know you have heard them and have done something about it. You will be amazed at the positive response – get ready for them to share their positive feelings about your company with their friends!

OTHER INTEGRATION POINTS

We've talked about how Social Customer Care can integrate with the rest of the Customer Service team, with Marketing, and with Products and Engineering teams. Where else can it integrate? The answer is really anywhere.

"I've always believed that social media needs to be deeply integrated into every business function and every business unit and that it shouldn't stand alone as a separate item," said Conversocial's Joshua March. "It needs to be deeply integrated into how you do marketing and the rest of your digital marketing efforts. It needs to be deeply integrated into how you do Customer Service or how you do sales, how you do research and consumer research. And the value of deep integration in any one of those areas, especially all of them, far outweighs trying to have a social tool that does everything social that isn't being integrated into [the] business."[15]

11

INTEGRATION WITH CRM
(WINNING AT SOCIAL CUSTOMER CARE STEP #8)

Ladies and Gentlemen, we've come to the part of the book where we will now talk about the "Holy Grail" of social Customer Service. Whereas Integration With the Core Business, which we discussed in the last chapter, is very difficult because it involves strong collaboration across multiple areas of the business, this final step represents the ultimate experience for both brands and customers. To be honest, of the dozens of brands we have interviewed for the *Focus on Customer Service* podcast, only one – Telstra in Australia – claimed to have achieved Holy Grail status.

WHAT IS IT?

Integration with CRM represents the flipside of the last chapter. Now we are going to use the Voice of the Customer to influence *that* customer's future experiences with the brand. In other words, the brand will remember previous conversations and requests from the customer and proactively act on them in *all* future interactions.

For example, imagine a customer who asks for a hypo-allergenic pillow at the front desk of a hotel in London. A month later, when he's using Facebook Messenger to ask the same hotel chain about availability in New York City, the agent confirms his reservation and, without him asking, tells him that his hypo-allergenic pillow will be waiting. Magic!

The key to success here is that we must be channel agnostic – a customer may ask us something on the phone, follow up with an email, and then send us a Facebook Messenger message weeks later. It shouldn't matter.

"It's really about how do we unify the customer experience, make sure that we have the context there and a customer doesn't even have to remember which communication channel they should use," said Sparkcentral's Davy Kestens. "They should just find you and talk to you. And that's a problem that hasn't really been solved."[1]

At the simplest level, a CRM (which stands for "Customer Relationship Management") system should be able to do this. But most CRM systems were built for telephone only, with maybe email and click-to-chat bolted on later. Many CRM systems are "home grown" or unique to one company, making additions and improvements that much more cumbersome. Data is often incomplete; companies have been collecting customer email addresses for years yet most still have only a fraction of their customers' emails on file.

Social media caused an additional layer of complication to CRM systems because except for Facebook, most social media platforms don't require that people use their real names. Companies, therefore, have been slow to integrate social media profiles into their CRM systems.

THREE FACETS OF CRM INTEGRATION

There are three main facets to CRM integration that need to be addressed:

Technology: Most of the Technology providers that we discussed in Chapter 5 are standalone products, meaning they may or may not directly interact with an existing CRM system. Even for ones that say they integrate with common CRM platforms like Salesforce, it is usually not as simple as "flipping a switch." Home-grown systems may be much more complex to develop integration with, especially if they don't have existing API's (Application Programming Interface). As a result, you may have to "special order" that integration with a (potentially costly) joint project between the vendor and your internal technology team.

Alternatively, you may be able to begin the process of manually collecting social data as customers interact with you. This clearly faces the same barriers as email collection. Still, as more and more customers move toward social channels as a primary method for Customer Service interactions, it may only be necessary to ensure institutional memory of a customer's interactions there. Most of the Technology providers we reviewed will maintain conversational history within individual social media platforms, so then all that is required is training your agents to take the extra few moments to review that history before responding to a new inquiry.

Data Collection: What information do you need to collect from your customer in order to recognize them and their previous requests in the future? First you will need an identifier, like an account number or loyalty number. You will also need access to your customers' frequent requests, patterns, or even general interests. Let's look at these separately:

Frequent requests: This is the hypo-allergenic pillow example, where a customer has specifically asked for something in the past. Other hotel examples include: food allergies or preferences, a high or low floor near or far from the elevator, a wheelchair-accessible room, a crib, or a filled ice bucket.

Patterns: This is a step further, whereby the hotel notices certain things about the customer without the customer actually specifying. Examples include: a frequent traveler who always arrives late at night to the hotel; one who always arrives with a set of golf clubs; one who always eats at the breakfast buffet or orders a late-night cheeseburger; one who visits the fitness center every afternoon.

General Interests: A quick look at Google or social media could result in a treasure trove of additional information, including occupation, hobbies, and favorite sports teams. The hotel doesn't have to use all of this information directly (alas, it may seem too "big brother" to do so) but it definitely can put together a well-rounded view of a frequent customer in order to provide him or her with better service.

Data Activation: The information you collect about your customers is not worth anything unless you can act on it. Now let's revisit the data we just collected and consider how we might activate it to make our customers' experience with our brand even more memorable:

Frequent requests: Whether the customer has asked for it once or many times, the hotel chain can and should leverage these requests in future interactions and assume that the customer will need the hypo-allergenic pillow again in his or her high-floor room near the elevator.

Patterns: The traveler who checks in late is likely arriving on a late flight and is tired from traveling. The hotel chain could proactively do one or more of the following: Automatically arrange for a late check-in for all visits; have the customer's room keys ready when he or she arrives in order to bypass the check-process; have the bed turned down knowing he or she is likely going right to bed; or arrange for housekeeping to make up the room late in the morning so as not to disturb the guest if he or she sleeps late. A fitness buff may appreciate an extra bottle of water, and the frequent diner may like a free appetizer or a discount coupon to the hotel's restaurant.

General Interests: Without watching social media, the Amelia Island Residence Inn would have never known that Eric Tung liked chocolate bars and drawings of pickles. Customers who have posted about their experience with your brand on social media are also providing feedback on what they liked (and maybe didn't like), which can be used to adjust the experience in the future. And other general interest information can be used to surprise and delight a customer; for example, if a hotel knew I love pinball and happened to have an arcade, they could proactively let me know at check in and maybe even provide some quarters!

CRM integration also brings together all Customer Service channels into a single authoritative record of each customer's experience (at least as far as service is concerned).

"It is essential for social media to be fully integrated into the contact center," notes Conversocial in its *Definitive Guide*. "This allows agents to be managed and resourced properly, with the same efficiency metrics as other channels, and with integration of data across different channels – allowing a customer to move seamlessly between social, email and phone if necessary."[2]

PERSONALIZATION

When you personalize or customize the experience to each individual customer, you make it that much more memorable. You may hate pinball, so telling you about the arcade at the hotel would have little effect whereas I would be disappointed if they *didn't* tell me.

"The general consensus across both marketing and service channels is that customers are seeking more personalized experiences and social is the channel where companies can best show that they are human, responsive and alert to customers' concerns," says Conversocial's *Definitive Guide*. "The value of social isn't limited to the customer-facing aspects. On the backend, social provides valuable data to glean patterns in customer behavior, communication, and recurring complaints."[3]

Personalization can take many forms, the simplest of which (in social media, anyway) is addressing customers by their names and signing responses with the agent's name or initials. This one small act serves to humanize the experience in a way that a Twitter handle alone cannot. But that's just the beginning.

"Personalization is becoming huge," said Shep Hyken. "Companies need to mine the data they have on each individual customer to give them a better customer experience. We have the data, and now we're the getting capability that allows us to use it easier and better than ever."[4]

Telstra, Australia's largest telecommunications company, has taken personalization to a level not seen by any other brand I am aware of. Monty Hamilton explains:

"We want all customer interactions to acknowledge the customer's name but most importantly offer our individual names in those interactions," he said. "That enables us to, whatever channel that dialogue takes place in, help customers connect with the same person for any particular problem or inquiry that they've got... We do that not only via telephone, we do it in our stores, we do in our social media footprint, and we also do it via live chat which is an enormous Customer Service channel for us."[5]

Wait, did he just say that customers can actually reconnect with the same Customer Service agent who they talked with before?

"Absolutely," said Hamilton. "And why that's important is that a lot of frustration stems from customers having to re-tell their story... it can be quite frustrating to repeat your situation or repeat the problem or inquiry that you've got."[6]

That's amazing, right? Telstra clearly has a robust and completely integrated CRM system (and some way of both training agents on multiple service channels and strategically planning their availability), but the actual implementation to the customer is fairly simple: "At the end of each telephone call or the end of a chat session, we simply send an email to the customer and it enables the customer to reconnect with the particular team member or colleague of mine that helped them out with their inquiry in the first place."[7]

Needless to say, Telstra has seen extraordinary success with this level of personalization.

"It is a real game changer for us," said Hamilton, "and our customers are loving it."[8]

12

THE PROLIFERATION OF MESSAGING APPS

There is no question that social media Customer Service is heading toward messaging as the core vehicle. In fact, four of the top five social media platforms by number of users worldwide are messaging apps, per Statista.[1] They are, in order: Facebook, WhatsApp, Facebook Messenger, QQ, and WeChat. There are more than 5 billion people using those five platforms. Comparatively, big names like Twitter, Snapchat, LinkedIn, and Pinterest are many times smaller.

"Messaging is an organic interface for a customer to ask for anything on-demand in a private, personal environment that truly replicates a concierge model," says Artificial Intelligence (AI) platform msg.ai in its white paper entitled, *Conversational Interfaces: Messaging as the New Browser.* "Messaging could also take most of the pain away from today's Customer Service experience."[2]

Sparkcentral's Davy Kestens said he has definitely noticed a change with his clients.

"What we've already seen over the last few years is a large amount of interactions through social media, for instance Twitter, have already been moving from the public channels to direct messages," he said. "Now the core set of people that are using social for customer care already realize that brands are listening and actually move to DM as soon as possible to create more of a one-to-one personal, concierge-level messaging experience within social channels."[3]

This is fascinating given that the whole uniqueness of social media for Customer Service lies in the fact that it is public. Messaging platforms are instead private channels, but in fact can be more human and engaging. This is potentially good news for brands, because fewer complaints may appear in public social media channels.

Conversocial's Joshua March believes that messaging apps are "the future of Customer Service."[4] His argument is that messaging apps have two main advantages over "traditional" social media: they're private (which brands love because it keeps complaints out of the public eye) and they're persistent (which customers love because they don't have to repeat their problem or even their account information to multiple agents).

March describes this evolving phenomenon:

"Messaging output has completely blown up from the consumer perspective; they really become the dominant way that consumers interact with each other and communicate with each other," he said. "Whether that's WhatsApp, which in much of the world has just replaced SMS, whether it's Facebook Messenger, whether it's Snapchat, whatever it is, these channels are now bigger than social networks, bigger than SMS, and if you look at the younger generation, completely dwarf things like email and phone calls as well.

"From a service perspective they're really exciting in lots of ways," he added. "First of all, they have full live chat capabilities, and as a lot of business know – especially in the contact center – if you can deliver live chat to a customer, it's highly efficient from an agent perspective, [and] it's also a great experience; it often gets better CSAT [customer satisfaction] ratings than any other service channel including phone calls."[5]

March cites his client Sprint as a great case study. After launching Customer Service in Facebook Messenger, Sprint saw a 31% rise in volume on Messenger – but a somewhat surprising (and welcome) corresponding reduction in public complaints on Facebook! This is a win-win for both consumers and brands.

"I think we're going to see a lot more brands start to promote messaging as one of their primary service channels," March said.[6]

Another benefit of messaging platforms is that they all work the same way. This makes developing a Process (and training your agents) easier because each platform doesn't have as many nuances (character length, hashtag usage, etc.). In fact, the dedicated service providers outlined in Chapter 5 are quickly developing interfaces for agents to consolidate all messaging experiences. Agents may end up not even knowing which messaging platform the inquiry is coming from and can answer in a consistent way every time.

This is especially helpful because there are so many different messaging platforms, with many consumers having multiple messaging apps on their mobile devices with their own personalized system of using each one for a specific purpose.

"Consumers today are starting to fragment their own conversations with different target audiences or different organizations or different people across their own communication channels," said Kestens. "The way we as consumers communicate today is more and more gravitating towards messaging and brands are rather slow to adopt."[7]

And adopt they must, because the move from public to private channels has not decreased consumers' extremely high expectations of a seamless customer experience.

"This doesn't let brands off the hook for stellar, human service," notes the Conversocial *Definitive Guide*. "The social customer will keep one finger on the escalation button and one eye on the prize when dealing with you. If you will not resolve in-channel or respond quickly, those public takedowns of your brand are still on the table."[8]

Finally, messaging apps eliminate the back-and-forth of email or social media and replace it with real-time resolution. So as 24-hour response times in email have given way to an hour or less in social media, messaging apps essentially bring that time down to nearly zero. This is a great experience for customers.

But are messaging apps really "the future of Customer Service"? That's a bold statement, and upon hearing it I immediately wondered whether all the work brands have done to become good at Customer Service in other channels might end up for naught if March's prediction comes true.

That's not what he was saying, of course, but I can almost hear the collective anxiety/anticipation/gasping of brands saying, "Darn it, we finally figured out this Social Customer Care thing and now we have to pivot again to private messaging?"

The reality, though, is that many brands are already doing private messaging – in the form of click-to-chat on their website or mobile app. So maybe Messenger and WhatsApp are just extensions of that, but with the benefit of meeting customers where they are instead of waiting for them to come to us.

BOTS

With the massive growth of messaging for brand interactions has come an exciting yet potentially disturbing additional development: Customer Service "bots." In truth, bots have been around for a long time – in the form of Interactive Voice Response (IVR) systems on the phone and even some very basic automation on website click-to-chat services. But I will admit to being worried that robots have a chance to take over and reverse the progress that we've made on really strong, personalized Customer Service in public.

Who's excited about the social media version of "To hear your balance, press 1. To make a payment, press 2. If you know your party's extension, dial it now. To bang your head against the wall, press 9. To speak with a customer agent, press 0 and then wait on hold for an hour"? Certainly not I. The digitized version of this will most certainly need to be a better customer experience, and in theory that's where bots have an opportunity.

But as of this writing, they aren't there yet.

"Most bots that you see today basically replace that one-on-one personal conversation that consumers are looking for with a modern IVR where basically you go through a list of questions, the bot doesn't understand the context and doesn't know it when you talk off script or don't give them the exact responses that are proposed to them, and then the customer experience around it is very bad the moment you go off script or the moment you are asking questions it doesn't know how to handle," said Kestens. "I think that the whole reason a lot of consumers are using these communication channels is to talk to a human being. So you shouldn't be doing the exact opposite with bots."[9]

March agrees. "We are not at the stage yet where you can have a really comprehensive chat bot that would work for Customer Service," he said. "I'm actually pretty excited by the potential for AI to help add value in contact center platforms, supporting agents, making their lives easier and increasing their efficiencies, but we're a ways from having a real chat bot that is going to be effective to Customer Service probably by at least a couple of years."[10]

The opportunity is certainly there. Anyone who watched IBM's Watson destroy its human competition on *Jeopardy!*[11] knows that artificial intelligence is getting really sophisticated. The key is to also make it appear human.

"I think what's going to happen in the future is we're moving into the era of cognitive," said Shep Hyken, who had attended the IBM World of Watson conference just before recording a *Focus on Customer Service* podcast episode with me. "What Watson is doing and some other artificial intelligence systems are doing is they're not just retrieving information, knowing where to get it and how to assimilate it, to make it sound good to a human. They are actually thinking. They're truly going to learn about their customers, and every time they interact with us they're going to get even better and better."[12]

The best place to start with messaging bots is routine Customer Service inquiries, of which there are many. The reason why that IVR on your credit card company's toll-free number starts with "To hear your balance" is that millions of people call in for just that reason every year. Having the computer look up and respond to this very simple question is easier and cheaper for the company, and usually faster for the customer as well. If messaging bots can provide the same service with frequent or repetitive inquiries, it should result in a faster, easier customer experience for the consumer and a more efficient Process for the company, which can then focus its agents on more complex inquiries that need human interaction.

"What is the best customer experience we can build out of this?" asks Kestens. "Looking at Social Customer Care, looking at messaging and bots as a feature on top of it, it's really about how do we reduce the customer effort... zero effort creates great customer experience."[13]

The other place where bots can be of value is in support of the agent. Intelligence Augmentation, or IA, is sort of the reverse of AI. Instead of the bot taking over, it assists the agent in delivering a human response to the customer. Imagine an agent having a Watson-like companion constantly at his or her side which can look up customer information and answers to millions of questions in a fraction of the time the agent can? Then the agent is still there to provide actual human engagement.

Artificial Intelligence platform msg.ai notes in its *Conversational Interfaces* white paper that there are obvious benefits of messaging bots[14]:

For Consumers:

- Highly personal support instantly
- All communication kept within a single thread, eliminating the need to dig up multiple emails or notes from calls
- The need for calls and interaction via other customer support channels is eliminated
- Anytime, anywhere communication on the app(s) that they are using every day.

For Brands:

- Effectively engage with their customers on mobile
- Better nurture relationships
- Drive loyalty through better customer experiences
- Decrease operational costs if artificial intelligence is leveraged to automate most of the interaction

But brands must be careful to not introduce an experience that is meant to simplify yet ends up complicating. As March points out: "So many businesses we work with are really trying to go under a digital transformation, where they want to move all these volumes away from phone calls which are often really expensive and sometimes a bad customer experience, into digital messaging channels where they can be cheaper and a better experience for customers… Why give them a potentially bad chat experience through a bot?"[15]

My personal fear is that too many companies will look at bots as a short-cut, a cost-saving opportunity that will result in "IVR hell" again, just on social media. Remember that social is a channel where the customer expectation is exactly the opposite of a robot; customers are craving a genuine personal conversation with a human being.

"There are some great systems out there that you don't know if you're dealing with a human or you're dealing with the robot," said Shep Hyken. "It doesn't matter as long as you don't know. It's if you know this is a canned response, this is what they say to everybody, it falls short."[16]

When your company is ready to experiment with messenger bots, be sure to work with a company that is well-integrated with the messaging platforms and their APIs. I was introduced to msg.ai directly by Facebook, which is a pretty good reference. The company's white paper offers 5 Rules for Messaging Success:

1. **Tailor Interaction to Context:** Brands should tap into contextual factors – the time of day, day of week, user location and weather conditions – to further tailor interaction, product recommendations, and offers. Furthermore, the tone and language of your conversation with a consumer will change based on various contextual factors, and will help the brand take on more of a friend role in a person's life.

2. **Exist across Marketing, Sales and Service:** The interaction on messaging apps should exist across the complete customer journey. Seamless 'hand off' between various divisions within your company should exist to provide a cohesive experience to customers.

3. **Leverage Human-Assisted AI and AI-Assisted Humans:** Consumers expect things on-demand; if there is a sizable lag before a brand responds to a message, consumers will quickly become disenchanted. Wherever possible, brands should leverage artificial intelligence to automate conversations... Some customer inquiries and conversations, though, are much better handled by a human... Have a system in place where the machine can hand off a conversation to human Customer Service personnel for these more sensitive scenarios to never compromise the user experience.

4. **Extend Engagement Through Personalized Content:** Treating chat like an email inbox will not do you any good, but after asking a customer's permission, sending relevant, personalized information and experiences via the chat thread will drive engagement. Map out scenarios in which you can organically participate in your customers' lives, without being spammy.

5. **Create a Community:** Allow people to share content…Additionally, allowing people to invite friends to join the conversation (like a group chat) further plays into natural consumer behavior and desire for involving those close to them in decisions.[17]

To summarize this section, messaging apps are here to stay, and they offer a lot of benefits to both consumers and brands. In the past, if brands wanted to engage in online chat with their customers, it needed to be on their own properties, i.e., their website or mobile app. Today, brands can chat with customers on the apps their customers are already using. This is one step closer to a brand truly being part of a consumer's life.

The good news is, everything you've learned in this book – and all of the Winning at Social Customer Care Steps – applies to messaging apps as well. It's just one more channel, worth separating into its own chapter because of its private nature and relative "newness" compared to the now-"traditional" social media platforms.

It is still too early to tell how the bot story ends. The technology will keep getting better, and with that will come improved customer experiences. It is certainly good enough today to try executing on simple customer experiences (checking an account balance, for example), and I definitely think that the IA model warrants further exploration – especially if it can remove some of the mundane tasks that agents are required to do, so they can spend more time interacting with customers.

Resist the urge to ask bots to do everything, because neither your customers nor your agents will thank you.

13

OTHER SOCIAL CUSTOMER CARE CHANNELS

While most of this book has focused on "traditional" social media platforms like Twitter and Facebook, and we have now covered the rise of messaging apps, the internet provides almost limitless opportunities for customers to engage with brands. Truthfully, I am less experienced in some of these other areas, but thankfully I know (and have interviewed) many people smarter than I when it comes to these other channels.

Two channels that we will cover briefly are Communities and Ratings and Reviews sites.

COMMUNITIES

Online communities have been around for a long time, but only a few brands have really changed customer behavior enough to drastically change the cost equation.

One that comes to mind for me is Intuit, which has had a Turbo Tax community[1] for years that is integrated right into the software. Users can both ask tax-related questions (because there are a lot of accountants in the community) and software-related questions (because there are a lot of users in the community). Conversations are "threaded," that is, organized into categories, and retained presumably for eternity because lots of questions get asked again and again.

Fitbit also has a vibrant user community, which Allison Leahy helped launch.

"It was really through blogging that I started to notice the power of online comments and user engagement and develop an interest in the psychological aspects of online community," said Leahy. "In particular, what happens when you carve out spaces for debate and self-expression and even support spaces for brands and companies online."[2]

Community platforms are used "as a way to organize information around emerging issues and to troubleshoot and gather information from customers who may be experiencing a certain type of issue so that we can get a good assessment and bring that back to our engineering teams," added Leahy.[3]

Fitbit employs a bilateral approach to online customer care, focusing separately on social media and communities, though both groups report up through the same department. While Leahy considers the two channels "different disciplines" with different tools (and hence different agents), one similarity is that Fitbit does a lot of customer listening in both. The team has a system to "incorporate all of our great customer feedback into the products and services we develop," she said.[4] Her team shares weekly quantitative and qualitative feedback with the product and engineering teams, and the most popular ideas get integrated into future product releases.

In a way, communities combine the best elements of public social media channels and private messaging channels. "Community is really where we have more time and attention from users," Leahy said. "It's also more of a one-to-many platform, and our community forums are really rooted in a peer-to-peer support philosophy."[5]

Companies with community forums can monitor, moderate, and engage when necessary, but established communities can run almost by themselves much of the time because customers can self-serve.

"We're constantly impressed with the wealth of knowledge and expertise our users bring to the table," said Leahy. "They're often the best suited to answer each other's questions and motivate each other to get the most of their Fitbit experience. So our moderation team is really there to keep an eye on all unanswered topics, make sure any new topics posted get a response within 24 hours, and jump in whenever specific issues arise or when their troubleshooting skills or support expertise is needed."[6]

Not surprisingly, communities tend to draw different types of questions than "traditional" social media channels.

"Facebook and Twitter are typically folks that are having issues at the moment that just want to be heard," said Amy Bivin of Dell.[7] In contrast, the Dell Community Forum often features more complex or esoteric questions, sometimes from owners of older legacy systems.

Dell also leverages a group it calls "Dell Community Forum Rock Stars," which answers about 30% of inquiries, with Bivin's team ensuring that questions without an answer from the community are properly addressed.

"It's a great community," Bivin said. "They are expert users and each of them has different specialties and they just enjoy helping other people."[8] The Rock Stars aren't paid, but they do enjoy certain perks like early access to new products and occasionally the ability to meet Dell executives.

Another benefit of communities? They can provide great content for both the Marketing and Customer Service departments, even driving SEO (Search Engine Optimization) value.

"If we can get people really reading our content on our help site and on the community forums first, we have even a greater chance of call deflection and customers are always happier if they don't have to contact you at all," said Fitbit's Leahy.[9]

At Dell, the community has generated so much content over time that SEO drives a ton of traffic to the forum, with customers often Googling "Dell" and a question about their product and being directed straight to the Forum.

Agents in other Customer Service channels also leverage the community's answers. "We want to drive folks there so that they can self-solve online," Dell's Bivin explains.[10]

The future of communities may actually lie in the integration with social media. Conversocial's Joshua March said that a few brands are testing this integration, allowing peer "experts" to answer customers' questions on social media from their own personal Twitter handles, rather than the brand answering. This definitely has potential in the future if it can be effectively scaled.

"There have been online communities of people helping each other for probably decades," said March. "How can we help take these communities which are just so powerful and unleash them into the social mobile world?"[11]

Another Intuit brand, QuickBooks, which caters to small businesses, has begun the integration with social media by participating in existing private communities on those channels.

"There was a lot of conversation happening on non-owned channels," explains Mark Obee, group manager of Social and Community Care for Intuit on the QuickBooks brand. "The accountants were out there having those conversations without us."[12]

Non-owned channels include private Facebook and LinkedIn groups, which caused a dilemma for a big company like Intuit. Obee knew that these sorts of groups were private for a reason – they didn't want big brands infiltrating with unwanted marketing messages.

Obee and his team reached out to influencers within these groups and asked how they could help. His goal was to "participate in those conversations to drive better outcomes." He quickly honed in on the answer: "listen, engage, and answer questions" with "honesty and transparency" – and no marketing.[13]

"We learned that coming in as a participant versus an advocate, we were able to actually gain the trust of the groups," Obee said.[14] The Social Evangelism Program at Intuit's QuickBooks was born, and it has allowed the company to connect with some of its most engaged users and deliver feedback to the Products and Customer Service teams.

Discussions certainly revolved around QuickBooks, but they also extended to general questions about running a small business. Unpaid users eagerly engage with answers to both, and the QuickBooks team jumps in when necessary. It's important to "meet [customers] where they want to have those conversations," said Obee. "They won't always come to owned channels."[15]

The private groups have evolved into a complementary piece of the Customer Service ecosystem; QuickBooks still receives plenty of inquiries in social media, but they also use social channels to highlight the groups, leverage answers, and create additional engagement.

RATINGS AND REVIEWS SITES

There are many ratings and reviews sites available to consumers. Some of them, like Yelp, Google Reviews, and the membership-required Angie's List, cover many different industries. Others, like TripAdvisor (travel, entertainment, restaurants), Cruise Critic (cruises), or Edmunds (automobiles), cater to specific industries.

There are a few things that make ratings and reviews sites more complicated than "traditional" social media:

- There are lots of them, with varying degrees of reliability
- Some sites do not allow companies to post or respond to reviews
- Some sites allow reviewers to remain anonymous, making it very difficult for companies to follow up
- Many sites do not have APIs that Technology providers can utilize like they can for Facebook, Twitter, or messaging platforms

If you are able to respond on a particular site, then follow the same principles outlined in this book.

Scott Wise of Scotty's Brewhouse responds to Yelp and other restaurant review sites whenever possible:

"We monitor those sites and we go to them and if we see that we have a bad post... we'll look at them and then we reply below it and say, 'Hey, we apologize, we made a mistake, here's our Customer Service email address, send us a message so that we can take care of you,'" he said. "We always make sure that we send them some freebies and some free coupons and gift cards to say, 'Hey, give us another shot. Don't let this one experience shape and mold your view of my restaurant. Give me a second chance to make a first impression.'"[16]

And just like in social media, don't be afraid of complaints. Customer Service expert Shep Hyken notes that "a perfect five from a number of customers is not as powerful as a four point three, four point four. Perfect is not realistic. And when there's imperfect and you see how a company manages it, that's realistic. That's really great feedback to see."[17]

For more on ratings and reviews, and reputation management in general, I recommend Daniel Lemin's book, *Manipurated*[18].

14

THE FUTURE OF SOCIAL CUSTOMER CARE

So what happens next? It's anyone's guess, but social media, messaging apps, and artificial intelligence are here to stay. What companies do with them is still unclear. But if you've read this book and adopted the Winning at Social Customer Care Steps in your organization, you will be set up for success no matter what happens.

Why am I so confident about that? Because Customer Service is also here to stay, and companies will still need to meet or exceed customer expectations no matter what the communication method looks like.

The future of Customer Service is that the pie is expanding. Customers now have far more options to complain/compliment/ask questions than ever before, and their clear expectation is that brands will answer their questions wherever and whenever they are asked.

"The communication that consumers are having over these channels is merely the most prominent example of how the expectations and the behavior of the modern consumer has changed," said Sparkcentral's Davy Kestens. "And so social was the first wave of that; now the whole mobile messaging explosion worldwide is the second wave of that. But it's not going to stop there... Enterprises need to start figuring out how they can change their internal operations to reduce the amount of effort that customers have to put to get issues resolved. And that's really the bigger challenge."[1]

The good news for brands is that channels like Twitter offer lower-cost alternatives to traditional Customer Service channels like the telephone, and that customers are willing to spend more with brands who respond to

Customer Service inquiries on Twitter. And with both Twitter and Facebook investing heavily in Customer Service functionality, the brand and customer experience on both is only getting better. It does remain to be seen, however, whether other social media channels follow suit.

MARKETING YOUR CUSTOMER SERVICE

Some brands have even begun marketing social media as a Customer Service destination. This started with casual references in the "Contact Us" section of the company website, but recently some companies have become more vocal about actually encouraging customers to use the world's most public Customer Service channel.

In late 2015, Delta started running print advertisements that promised "No tweet unanswered."

"The next time you have a question during your journey," the ad said, "reach out to us on Twitter using @DeltaAssist [now just @Delta]. We're committed to responding within the hour."[2]

At Discover, my philosophy was that the company was so good at Customer Service, it might as well shout it from the rooftops. In this way, Customer Service actually becomes a form of marketing, as prospects and other customers witness superior service out in the open and form positive opinions of the company. It can actually become a competitive advantage.

"One of the biggest hesitations a lot of the companies have had in promoting social as a primary service channel has been the very public aspect of it," said Conversocial's Joshua March. "[But] if they're delivering a great experience, they see value in having that public and having other customers see that."[3]

Fitbit's Allison Leahy said the company looks at customer satisfaction (CSAT) scores to determine which Customer Service channels to promote.

"Social is definitely a high CSAT channel and it's also a great channel from a business standpoint because cost per contact is a little lower than some of the other channels," she said.[4] Twitter and the community forum are highlighted on the Fitbit website alongside "traditional" channels like telephone, email, and chat.

WHAT'S NEXT

Most brands that I've interviewed aren't seeing drastic reductions in Customer Service phone calls yet; in fact, for many companies social media is still a tiny fraction of overall Customer Service inquiries.

Yes, Millennials and their general distaste for the telephone and email may eventually move the needle toward social channels, but for now those two old "distasteful" channels are still by far the biggest for many brands. This is why the Customer Service pie must be expanding – there are so many new ways for customers to connect with brands today, yet the old-fashioned channels still remain incredibly popular.

One big difference is that customers are now bringing up issues, providing feedback or asking questions that they never would have previously, in part because it's so much easier to do so. In the past, customers called brands only when they were having problems. Today, they desire a personalized relationship with a brand even before they buy, and once they become a customer they want their ideas and suggestions to be heard. Smart brands seize the inherent opportunity in this change by using that feedback to continuously improve their products and experience.

Ultimately, it's going to be the customer that continues to drive change; brands will just have to go along for the ride. Now that customers have found their voice, they are not likely to give it up any time soon. New technology, new platforms, increasingly complex products, and the same old struggle to find enough time in the day will keep service expectations high. Customers will not tolerate poor Customer Service or a bad customer experience, and if you're not going to "wow" them, I promise there will be another company that will.

No matter what the size of your company is – or the size of your Social Customer Care team – you have the power to make a difference in your customers' lives. Always be that person in the room with the "customer hat" on; don't settle for corporate policies or antiquated procedures that don't put the customer first. Use the Winning at Social Customer Care Steps that you have learned in this book and heed the advice of the best-in-class brands you have heard from, and the future is yours to conquer. I thank you, and your customers will thank you.

ACKNOWLEDGEMENTS

For a man of many words, it is difficult for me to find the right ones to adequately show appreciation for all those who have helped this book come to life.

First and foremost, to my family: Thank you for putting up with me while I sequestered myself in the office, listening to podcast episodes and constantly typing away on the computer. I could not have done this without your love, patience, and flexibility.

Thanks to my parents for always encouraging me to believe in myself and pursue my passions.

To all of the amazing guests I've been fortunate to interview on the *Focus on Customer Service* podcast: I learned something from each and every one of you, even if you weren't quoted in the book. It is such a privilege to be able to talk with and learn from some of the top brands in the world – all while discussing a topic about which we share a mutual passion.

Special thanks to a select group of marketing, customer service, and social media influencers who have shown me so much respect and friendship by listening and advising as I've attempted to establish my own little corner of the social world. Much appreciation for the counsel provided by Jay Baer, John R. DiJulius III, Shep Hyken, Bryan Kramer, and Neal Schaffer. I'd also like to recognize the late Robin Carey for believing in me and agreeing to host and promote my podcast on *Social Media Today* before the first episode was ever recorded; and Phil Mershon of *Social Media Examiner* for trusting me to lead the first-ever Customer Service track at the iconic Social Media Marketing World conference.

To two bosses, both of whom influenced me to write this book in different ways: Mike Boush of Discover challenged me to become a "recognized expert" in digital and/or social media even though I was new to both disciplines; Jeff Reid of Humana challenged me to write down a personal goal and the steps I would take to achieve it within a year. Not surprisingly, my goal was to write a book.

To those who helped get this book to print: Dan Moriarty, my original co-host for the *Focus on Customer Service* podcast and the co-creator of the outline for the "8 Steps to Winning at Social Customer Care"; RJ Basilio, our awesome audio producer for the podcast; my brother and Pulitzer Prize-winning journalist, Jerry Markon, for editing the manuscript; Jay Baer (again!) for graciously agreeing to write the Foreword; and our cat Powder, who almost never left my lap while I wrote the book.

All episodes of the *Focus on Customer Service* podcast are available in their entirety on iTunes, Stitcher, SoundCloud, and wherever you listen to podcasts.

Please visit www.winningatsocial.com for more great content, and continue the discussion with me on Twitter at @dgingiss. Hopefully you'll find my Response Time to be best-in-class!

PHOTOS AND CHARTS

CHAPTER 1

"Compound average revenue growth, 2010-2015" chart courtesy of Forrester and used with permission.

"Quality service that doesn't cut corners is our recipe" photo by Dan Gingiss.

"We cannot provide any courtesy cups" photo by Dan Gingiss.

"Assistance available when 2 cashiers on duty" photo by Dan Gingiss.

Garbage receptacle photo by Melissa Douros and used with permission.

Garbage receptacle with tray photo by Melissa Douros and used with permission.

Iron under faucet photos 1 and 2 by Dan Gingiss.

Device plug under seat photo by Dan Gingiss.

Device plug inside tray table photo by Dan Gingiss.

CHAPTER 2

"Social media has turned customer service upside down" image by Dan Gingiss, quote by John R. DiJulius III.

Canadian telecom chat screenshot by Brian Fraser and used with permission.

Eric Tung chocolate and pickle image by Eric T. Tung. <https://twitter.com/EricTTung/status/580848471340552192> Used with permission. Accessed 14 Jan. 2017.

CHAPTER 3

"I would have waited 2 hours" image by Dan Gingiss.

Spotify playlist image courtesy of Spotify and used with permission.

Eric Tung chocolate and pickle 2 image by Eric T. Tung. <https://twitter.com/EricTTung/status/583070611620159488> Used with permission. Accessed 14 Jan. 2017.

CHAPTER 7

Scotty's Brewhouse training card image courtesy of Scott Wise and used with permission.

CHAPTER 9

"Cost per Resolution" calculation image by Dan Gingiss.

"Brand and Consumer Index Spotlight by Industry: Q3 2016" chart courtesy of Sprout Social and used with permission.

NOTES

CHAPTER 1

[1] Leahy, Allison. "Episode 44 - How Fitbit Keeps Its Customers Moving in Social Media and Online Communities." Interview with Dan Gingiss. *Focus on Customer Service* podcast. 28 Nov. 2016. Accessed 14 Jan. 2017.

[2] Wise, Scott. "Episode 17 – Scotty's Brewhouse." Interview with Dan Gingiss & Dan Moriarty. *Focus on Customer Service* podcast. 26 Oct. 2015. Accessed 14 Jan. 2017.

[3] Hyken, Shep. "Episode 45 - A Customer Service Expert on How Social Media Has Changed The Game (Shep Hyken)." Interview with Dan Gingiss. *Focus on Customer Service* podcast. 13 Dec. 2016. Accessed 14 Jan. 2017.

[4] "The $62 billion customer service scared away," *NewVoiceMedia*. 24 May 2016. <http://www.newvoicemedia.com/en-us/news/the-62-billion-customer-service-scared-away>. Accessed 14 Jan. 2017.

[5] Hyken, *Focus on Customer Service* podcast.

[6] Wise, *Focus on Customer Service* podcast.

[7] Hyken, *Focus on Customer Service* podcast.

[8] DiJulius, John R., III. *The Customer Service Revolution*. Austin, TX: Greenleaf Book Group, 2015.

[9] Schmidt-Subramanian, Maxine, et al. "The Business Impact Of Customer Experience, 2014." Forrester, 27 Mar. 2014. <https://www.forrester.com/report/The+Business+Impact+Of+Customer+Experience+2014/-/E-RES113421?objectid=RES113421>. Accessed 14 Jan. 2017.

[10] Manning, Harley. "Customer Experience Drives Revenue Growth, 2016." Forrester, 21 Jun. 2016. <http://blogs.forrester.com/harley_manning/16-06-21-customer_experience_drives_revenue_growth_2016> Accessed 14 Jan 2017.

[11] "ISO 9241, Section 2.15 - User Experience." International Organization for Standardization. (c) 2010. < https://www.iso.org/obp/ui/#iso:std:iso:9241:-210:ed-1:v1:en> Accessed 22 Jan. 2017.

CHAPTER 2

1   DiJulius, *The Customer Service Revolution.*

2   March, Joshua. "Episode 35 - Bridging the Gap Between Social Media and Customer Service." Interview with Dan Gingiss and Dan Moriarty. *Focus on Customer Service* podcast. 12 Jul. 2016. Accessed 14 Jan. 2017.

3   Hyken, *Focus on Customer Service* podcast.

4   *The Definitive Guide to Social, Mobile Customer Service: Volume 4, 2016-2017 Edition.* Conversocial, 2016.

5   Hamilton, Monty. "Episode 7 - Telstra." Interview with Dan Gingiss. *Focus on Customer Service* podcast. 28 Jul. 2015. Accessed 14 Jan. 2017.

6   Mattson, Michelle. "Episode 28 - How T-Mobile Brings Its "Un-Carrier" Image to Social Media." Interview with Dan Gingiss and Dan Moriarty. *Focus on Customer Service* podcast. 27 Mar. 2016. Accessed 14 Jan. 2017.

7   Wise, *Focus on Customer Service* podcast.

8   Ibid.

9   Mattson, *Focus on Customer Service* podcast.

10 Gingiss, Dan. "From Baseball to Business: How 'Maddonisms' Drive Success." *Purematter,* 20 Oct. 2016. <http://www.purematter.com/from-baseball-to-business-how-maddonisms-drive-success/> Accessed 14 Jan. 2017.

11 Cornell, Alex. *I'm on Hold,* 2014. <https://www.youtube.com/watch?v=zh9h4KZpnJU> Accessed 14 Jan. 2017.

12 Courtesy of iflix and used with permission.

13 Wise, *Focus on Customer Service* podcast.

CHAPTER 3

1   Conversocial, *The Definitive Guide to Social, Mobile Customer Service.*

2   *7 Steps to Kickstart A Social Customer Service Strategy: Start Your Engines.* Sparkcentral. <https://www.sparkcentral.com/resources/white-paper-seven-steps-to-kickstart/> Accessed 20 Jan. 2017.

3   Wise, *Focus on Customer Service* podcast.

4   Kestens, Davy. "Episode 42 - Solving Problems for Both Customers and Companies." Interview with Dan Gingiss and Dan Moriarty. *Focus on Customer Service* podcast. 24 Oct. 2016. Accessed 14 Jan. 2017.

5   Hyken, *Focus on Customer Service* podcast.

[6]   <https://twitter.com/amandacarpenter/status/698871105105346562>. Accessed 14 Jan. 2017.

[7]   Ibid.

[8]   Koerber, Brian. "Amtrak Asks Woman If She's Still Trapped in Elevator Months Later." Mashable, 08 Sept. 2016. <http://mashable.com/2016/09/08/amtrak-elevator-fail/#eLJdwLiMJqqc>. Accessed 14 Jan. 2017.

[9]   "Amtrak responds to woman stuck in elevator… seven months later." *The Today Show*, 12 Sep. 2016.   <http://www.today.com/video/amtrak-responds-to-woman-stuck-in-elevator-seven-months-later-762963523849>. Accessed 14 Jan. 2017.

[10]   <https://twitter.com/amandacarpenter/status/698871105105346562>. Accessed 14 Jan. 2017.

[11]   Tull, David. "Episode 21 - Jack Threads." Interview with Dan Gingiss and Dan Moriarty. *Focus on Customer Service* podcast. 22 Dec. 2015. Accessed 14 Jan. 2017.

[12]   Baer, Jay. *Hug Your Haters: How to Embrace Complaints and Keep Your Customers*. New York: Portfolio/Penguin, 2016.

[13]   Ibid.

[14]   Kramer, Bryan. *There Is No B2B or B2C: It's Human to Human: #H2H*. San Jose, CA: Purematter, 2014.

[15]   Kerpen, Dave, as quoted by Jay Baer in *Hug Your Haters: How to Embrace Complaints and Keep Your Customers*. New York: Portfolio/Penguin, 2016.

[16]   Baer, *Hug Your Haters*.

[17]   Ibid.

[18]   <https://twitter.com/RobSpeciale/status/311297618389127168> Accessed 14 Jan. 2017.

[19]   Ibid.

[20]   Ibid.

[21]   Abramowitz, Chug and Thomas, Sam. "Episode 31 - Spotify Is Hitting All The Right Notes in Social Customer Service." Interview with Dan Gingiss and Dan Moriarty. *Focus on Customer Service* podcast. 10 May 2016. Accessed 14 Jan. 2017.

CHAPTER 4

[1]   Wise, *Focus on Customer Service* podcast.

[2]   Hahn, Rob. "Episode 22 - Southwest Airlines." Interview with Dan Gingiss and Dan Moriarty. *Focus on Customer Service* podcast. 5 Jan. 2016. Accessed 14 Jan. 2017.

[3] <https://www.southwest.com/html/about-southwest/index. html?clk=GFOOTER-ABOUT-ABOUT> Accessed 14 Jan. 2017.

[4] Hamilton, *Focus on Customer Service* podcast.

[5] Wise, *Focus on Customer Service* podcast.

[6] Hamilton, *Focus on Customer Service* podcast.

[7] Ibid.

[8] "New Tools for Managing Communication on Your Page." Facebook Business, 8 Dec. 2015. <https://www.facebook.com/business/news/new-tools-for-managing-communication-on-your-page>. Accessed 14 Jan. 2017.

[9] Cairns, Ian. "Speed up Customer Service with Quick Replies & Welcome Messages in Direct Messages." Twitter Blog, 1 Nov. 2016. <https://blog.twitter.com/2016/speed-up-customer-service-with-quick-replies-welcome-messages-in-direct-messages>. Accessed 14 Jan. 2017.

[10] Kestens, *Focus on Customer Service* podcast.

[11] Ibid. (Moriarty commented during the Kestens interview.)

[12] March, *Focus on Customer Service* podcast.

[13] Ibid.

[14] Ibid.

[15] Hyken, *Focus on Customer Service* podcast.

[16] Baer, *Hug Your Haters.*

[17] Meacham, Laurie. "Episode 2 – JetBlue." Interview with Dan Gingiss and Dan Moriarty. *Focus on Customer Service* podcast. 15 Jun. 2015. Accessed 14 Jan. 2017.

[18] Huang, Wayne. "How Positive Customer Service Interactions on Twitter Boost Consumer Spending." Twitter Marketing, 7 Dec. 2015. <https://marketing.twitter.com/na/en/insights/customer-service-interactions-on-twitter-boost-consumer-spending.html>. Accessed 14 Jan. 2017.

[19] Huang, Wayne. "Episode 27 - Twitter Researcher Quantifies the ROI of Customer Service." Interview with Dan Gingiss and Dan Moriarty. *Focus on Customer Service* podcast. 15 Mar. 2016. Accessed 14 Jan. 2017.

[20] Ibid.

[21] Huang, Wayne. "Study: Twitter Customer Care Increases Willingness to Pay Across Industries." Twitter Blog, 5 Oct. 2106. <https://blog.twitter.com/2016/study-twitter-customer-care-increases-willingness-to-pay-across-industries>. Accessed 14 Jan. 2017.

[22] Anderson, Natanya. "Episode 1 - Whole Foods." Interview with Dan Gingiss and Dan Moriarty. *Focus on Customer Service* podcast. 8 Jun. 2015. Accessed 14 Jan. 2017.

[23] Miller, Nicole. "Episode 4 – Buffer." Interview with Dan Gingiss and Dan Moriarty. *Focus on Customer Service* podcast. 6 Jul. 2015. Accessed 14 Jan. 2017.

[24] Filmgraphics Entertainment. "Telstra 'Magda - Personal Service Promise.'" YouTube, 12 June 2014. <https://www.youtube.com/watch?v=h6DIdw8XIJQ>. Accessed 14 Jan. 2017.

[25] Hamilton, *Focus on Customer Service* podcast.

CHAPTER 5

[1] Kestens, *Focus on Customer Service* podcast.

[2] Ibid.

[3] Hahn, *Focus on Customer Service* podcast.

[4] March, *Focus on Customer Service* podcast.

[5] Mattson, *Focus on Customer Service* podcast.

[6] Conversocial, *The Definitive Guide to Social, Mobile Customer Service.*

[7] Kestens, *Focus on Customer Service* podcast.

[8] Conversocial, *The Definitive Guide to Social, Mobile Customer Service.*

[9] March, *Focus on Customer Service* podcast.

[10] Conversocial, *The Definitive Guide to Social, Mobile Customer Service.*

[11] Ibid.

[12] Hamilton, *Focus on Customer Service* podcast.

[13] Conversocial, *The Definitive Guide to Social, Mobile Customer Service.*

[14] Ibid.

CHAPTER 6

[1] DiJulius, John R., III. *What's The Secret?: To Providing a World-Class Customer Experience.* Hoboken, NJ: John Wiley & Sons, Inc., 2008.

[2] Mattson, *Focus on Customer Service* podcast.

[3] Ibid.

[4] "Tech Milestones in the Guinness World Records." CBS News. CBS Interactive, 22 Sept. 2011. <http://www.cbsnews.com/pictures/tech-milestones-in-the-guinness-world-records/12/>. Accessed 15 Jan. 2017.

[5]   Degnan, James. "Episode 19 – Xbox." Interview with Dan Gingiss and Dan Moriarty. *Focus on Customer Service* podcast. 24 Nov. 2015. Accessed 15 Jan. 2017.

[6]   Conversocial, *The Definitive Guide to Social, Mobile Customer Service.*

[7]   DiJulius, *The Customer Service Revolution.*

[8]   Meacham, *Focus on Customer Service* podcast

[9]   Conversocial, *The Definitive Guide to Social, Mobile Customer Service*

[10] Hahn, *Focus on Customer Service* podcast.

[11] Conversocial, *The Definitive Guide to Social, Mobile Customer Service*

[12] Wise, *Focus on Customer Service* podcast.

[13] Ibid.

[14] Bivin, Amy. "Episode 46 - How Dell's Community Forum Aids in Social Media Customer Service." Interview with Dan Gingiss. *Focus on Customer Service* podcast. 3 Jan. 2017. Accessed 15 Jan. 2017.

[15] Hyken, *Focus on Customer Service* podcast.

[16] Wise, *Focus on Customer Service* podcast.

[17] March, *Focus on Customer Service* podcast.

[18] Kestens, *Focus on Customer Service* podcast.

[19] Sparkcentral, *7 Steps to Kickstart A Social Customer Service Strategy.*

[20] Ibid.

[21] Conversocial, *The Definitive Guide to Social, Mobile Customer Service.*

[22] Leahy, *Focus on Customer Service* podcast.

[23] Piercy, Madeleine (née Aman). "Episode 33 - How The Largest Utility in the U.S. Helps Customers Weather the Storm in Social Media." Interview with Dan Gingiss. *Focus on Customer Service* podcast. 6 Jun. 2017. Accessed 15 Jan. 2017.

[24] Hahn, *Focus on Customer Service* podcast.

[25] Piercy, *Focus on Customer Service* podcast.

[26] Sparkcentral, *7 Steps to Kickstart A Social Customer Service Strategy.*

[27] Hyken, *Focus on Customer Service* podcast.

CHAPTER 7

[1]   Conversocial, *The Definitive Guide to Social, Mobile Customer Service*

[2]   Mattson, *Focus on Customer Service* podcast.

[3]   Hyken, *Focus on Customer Service* podcast.

[4]   Wise, *Focus on Customer Service* podcast.

[5]   <http://lmgtfy.com/>. Accessed 15 Jan. 2017.

[6]   Hamilton, *Focus on Customer Service* podcast.

[7]   Ibid.

[8]   Kapoor, Kriti. "Episode 20 - HP Inc." Interview with Dan Gingiss and Dan Moriarty. *Focus on Customer Service* podcast. 8 Dec. 2015. Accessed 15 Jan. 2017.

[9]   Mattson, *Focus on Customer Service* podcast.

[10]   Kestens, *Focus on Customer Service* podcast.

[11]   Sparkcentral, *7 Steps to Kickstart A Social Customer Service Strategy.*

[12]   Baer, *Hug Your Haters.*

CHAPTER 8

[1]   Hyken, *Focus on Customer Service* podcast.

[2]   In-person discussion with Dan Moriarty.

[3]   Hahn, *Focus on Customer Service* podcast.

[4]   Conversocial, *The Definitive Guide to Social, Mobile Customer Service.*

[5]   Hamilton, *Focus on Customer Service* podcast.

[6]   Mattson, *Focus on Customer Service* podcast.

[7]   Leahy, *Focus on Customer Service* podcast.

[8]   DON CIO Privacy Team. "What Is Personally Identifiable Information?" Department of Navy Chief Information Officer, 15 July 2011. <http://www.doncio. navy.mil/ContentView.aspx?id=2428>. Accessed 15 Jan. 2017.

[9]   "Guidance Regarding Methods for De-identification of Protected Health Information in Accordance with the Health Insurance Portability and Accountability Act (HIPAA) Privacy Rule." U.S. Department of Health & Human Services, 06 Nov. 2015. <https://www.hhs.gov/hipaa/for-professionals/privacy/special-topics/de-identification/#protected>. Accessed 15 Jan. 2017.

[10]   "Employee Rights." National Labor Relations Board. <https://www.nlrb.gov/rights-we-protect/employee-rights>. Accessed 15 Jan. 2017.

[11]   Gingiss, Dan. "United Airlines: Great Customer Service in the Midst of A Crisis." Social Media Today, 09 July 2015. <http://www.socialmediatoday.com/social-business/dgingiss/2015-07-09/united-airlines-great-customer-service-midst-crisis>. Accessed 15 Jan. 2017.

[12]   <https://twitter.com/united/status/618777538865799168>. Accessed 15 Jan. 2017.

[13]   <https://twitter.com/united/status/618789982468075520>. Accessed 15 Jan. 2017.

[14]   <https://twitter.com/united/status/618869380114354176>. Accessed 15 Jan. 2017.

[15]   Ibid.

[16]   DiJulius, *The Customer Service Revolution.*

[17]   Abramowitz and Thomas, *Focus on Customer Service* podcast.

[18]   Jesseau, Lindsay. "Episode 6 – Vega." Interview with Dan Gingiss and Dan Moriarty. *Focus on Customer Service* podcast. 21 Jul. 2015. Accessed 15 Jan. 2017.

[19]   Meacham, *Focus on Customer Service* podcast.

[20]   Saghy, Kevin. "Episode 26 - Cubs Win! The Most Engaging Team in Baseball." Interview with Dan Gingiss and Dan Moriarty. *Focus on Customer Service* podcast. 1 Mar. 2016. Accessed 15 Jan. 2017.

[21]   Piercy, *Focus on Customer Service* podcast.

[22]   Bivin, *Focus on Customer Service* podcast.

[23]   Sparkcentral, *7 Steps to Kickstart A Social Customer Service Strategy.*

[24]   Wise, *Focus on Customer Service* podcast.

[25]   Boone, Ashley. "Episode 5 – Modcloth." Interview with Dan Gingiss and Dan Moriarty. *Focus on Customer Service* podcast. 12 Jul. 2015. Accessed 15 Jan. 2017.

[26]   Hyken, *Focus on Customer Service* podcast.

[27]   DiJulius, *The Customer Service Revolution.*

[28]   Tull, *Focus on Customer Service* podcast.

[29]   Hyken, *Focus on Customer Service* podcast.

[30]   Mattson, *Focus on Customer Service* podcast.

[31]   Ibid.

[32]   Baer, *Hug Your Haters.*

[33]   "New Tools for Managing Communication on Your Page." Facebook Business, 8 Dec. 2015. <https://www.facebook.com/business/news/new-tools-for-managing-communication-on-your-page>. Accessed 15 Jan. 2017.

[34]   Basulto, David. "Episode 24 - iOgrapher, the startup using Snapchat as a customer service tool." Interview with Dan Gingiss and Dan Moriarty. *Focus on Customer Service* podcast. 2 Feb. 2016. Accessed 15 Jan. 2017.

[35]   Conversocial, *The Definitive Guide to Social, Mobile Customer Service.*

[36] Bivin, *Focus on Customer Service* podcast.

[37] Gingiss, Dan. "Delta Now Flying High With a Single Twitter Handle." Social Media Today, 20 Apr. 2016. <http://www.socialmediatoday.com/social-business/delta-now-flying-high-single-twitter-handle>. Accessed 15 Jan. 2017.

[38] Piercy, *Focus on Customer Service* podcast.

CHAPTER 9

[1] "Youtility: Why Smarter Marketing Is about Help, Not Hype." Salesforce Marketing Cloud (Webinar with Jay Baer), 07 Oct. 2014. <http://www.slideshare.net/marketingcloud/youtility-why-smarter-marketing-is-about-help-not-hype>. Accessed 15 Jan. 2017.

[2] Kestens, *Focus on Customer Service* podcast.

[3] "The Q4 2016 Sprout Social Index." Sprout Social. <http://sproutsocial.com/insights/data/q4-2016/>. Accessed 15 Jan. 2017.

[4] Conversocial, *The Definitive Guide to Social, Mobile Customer Service.*

[5] Mattson, *Focus on Customer Service* podcast.

[6] Hahn, *Focus on Customer Service* podcast

[7] Conversocial, *The Definitive Guide to Social, Mobile Customer Service.*

[8] Ibid.

[9] Gahagen, Krysta. "What's New with Twitter's Customer Support Features?" Sparkcentral. 6 Oct. 2016. <https://www.sparkcentral.com/blog/whats-new-twitters-customer-support-features/>. Accessed 25 Jan. 2017.

[10] Twitter for Customer Service Team, *Customer Service on Twitter, 2015 Edition.* San Francisco, CA: Twitter Inc., 2015.

[11] Sprout Social, "The Q4 2016 Sprout Social Index."

CHAPTER 10

[1] Martin, Todd. Live presentation at Incite Group's Corporate Social Media Summit, 20 Jun. 2016. Quoted on Twitter: <https://twitter.com/dgingiss/status/745004940955791360>. Accessed 15 Jan. 2017.

[2] Feloni, Richard. "A Zappos Employee Had the Company's Longest Customer-service Call at 10 Hours, 43 Minutes." *Business Insider*, 26 July 2016. <http://www.businessinsider.com/zappos-employee-sets-record-for-longest-customer-service-call-2016-7>. Accessed 15 Jan. 2017.

3 Baer, *Hug Your Haters.*

4 Wise, *Focus on Customer Service* podcast.

5 Baer, *Hug Your Haters.*

6 Ibid.

7 Leahy, *Focus on Customer Service* podcast.

8 DiJulius, *The Customer Service Revolution.*

9 Wise, *Focus on Customer Service* podcast.

10 Mack, Jessica. "Episode 9 – OtterBox." Interview with Dan Gingiss and Dan Moriarty. *Focus on Customer Service* podcast. 17 Aug. 2015. Accessed 15 Jan. 2017.

11 Jesseau, *Focus on Customer Service* podcast.

12 Leahy, *Focus on Customer Service* podcast.

13 Ibid.

14 Hyken, *Focus on Customer Service* podcast.

15 March, *Focus on Customer Service* podcast.

CHAPTER 11

1 Kestens, *Focus on Customer Service* podcast.

2 Conversocial, *The Definitive Guide to Social, Mobile Customer Service.*

3 Ibid.

4 Hyken, *Focus on Customer Service* podcast.

5 Hamilton, *Focus on Customer Service* podcast.

6 Ibid.

7 Ibid.

8 Ibid.

CHAPTER 12

1 "Global Social Media Ranking 2016." Statista, 2016. <https://www.statista.com/statistics/272014/global-social-networks-ranked-by-number-of-users/>. Accessed 15 Jan. 2017.

2 *Conversational Interfaces: Messaging as the New Browser.* msg.ai, 2016. <http://msg.ai/#features> Accessed 15 Jan. 2017.

3 Kestens, *Focus on Customer Service* podcast.

4 March, *Focus on Customer Service* podcast.

5 Ibid.

6   Ibid.

7   Kestens, *Focus on Customer Service* podcast.

8   Conversocial, *The Definitive Guide to Social, Mobile Customer Service.*

9   Kestens, *Focus on Customer Service* podcast.

10   March, *Focus on Customer Service* podcast.

11   Markoff, John. "Computer Wins on 'Jeopardy!': Trivial, It's Not." *The New York Times*, 16 Feb. 2011. <http://www.nytimes.com/2011/02/17/science/17jeopardy-watson.html>. Accessed 15 Jan. 2017.

12   Hyken, *Focus on Customer Service* podcast.

13   Kestens, *Focus on Customer Service* podcast.

14   msg.ai, *Conversational Interfaces: Messaging as the New Browser.*

15   March, *Focus on Customer Service* podcast

16   Hyken, *Focus on Customer Service* podcast.

17   msg.ai, *Conversational Interfaces: Messaging as the New Browser.*

CHAPTER 13

1   < https://turbotax.intuit.com/best-tax-software/why-choose-turbotax/help-live-community.jsp> Accessed 15 Jan. 2017.

2   Leahy, *Focus on Customer Service* podcast.

3   Ibid.

4   Ibid.

5   Ibid.

6   Ibid.

7   Bivin, *Focus on Customer Service* podcast.

8   Ibid.

9   Leahy, *Focus on Customer Service* podcast.

10   Bivin, *Focus on Customer Service* podcast.

11   March, *Focus on Customer Service* podcast.

12   Obee, Mark. "Episode 43 - How Intuit's QuickBooks Meets Its Small Business Customers Anywhere." Interview with Dan Gingiss. *Focus on Customer Service* podcast. 7 Nov. 2016. Accessed 15 Jan. 2017.

13   Ibid.

14   Ibid.

15   Ibid.

[16]   Wise, *Focus on Customer Service* podcast.

[17]   Hyken, *Focus on Customer Service* podcast.

[18]   Lemin, Daniel. *Manipurated: How Business Owners Can Fight Fraudulent Online Ratings and Reviews*. Fresno, CA: Quill Driver, 2015.

CHAPTER 14

[1]   Kestens, *Focus on Customer Service* podcast.

[2]   Lorenzetti, Laura. "Delta Will Respond to Your Thanksgiving Travel Mishaps Via Twitter." *Fortune*, 25 Nov. 2015. <http://fortune.com/2015/11/25/delta-travel-problem-response/>. Accessed 15 Jan. 2017.

[3]   March, *Focus on Customer Service* podcast.

[4]   Leahy, *Focus on Customer Service* podcast.

7 Steps To Kickstart A Social Customer Service Strategy 29, 66, 67, 70, 81, 94

8 Steps to Winning at Social Customer Care. 39

Abramson, Chug 34

Adobe. 54

airline industry. 45

American Airlines. 97

Amtrak. .31

Anderson, Natanya. 47

API (Application Programming Interface) 58, 80, 123, 134, 140

Apple 11

artificial intelligence . . 80, 128, 132, 133, 134, 141

Availability (24/7) 41, 42, 107

Baer, Jay 32, 33, 45, 81, 96, 97, 103, 115, 118

Basulto, David 97

Bivin, Amy. 64, 65, 94, 99, 138

Boone, Ashley 94

bots 53, 80, 131, 132, 133, 134, 135

Brand Embassy. 56

brand voice. 41, 48, 74

Buffer. 47, 48, 54

Carpenter, Amanda 31

chat (channel) . . 28, 29, 32, 60, 67, 85, 86, 109, 123, 129, 131, 142

Chicago Bulls. 43, 83

Chicago Cubs. 21, 93

Comcast. 97

communities . . .136, 137, 138, 139

community management . . . 80, 81, 112

complaints

    and process improvement. . . 99, 119, 126

    reducing. 20, 90, 115, 116, 129

    responding to. . . 32, 33, 45, 48, 50, 56, 76, 118

compliments, responding to 48, 95, 117, 141

conversation threads... 51, 54, 133, 136

Conversational Interfaces: Messaging as the New Browser 128, 133

Conversocial. 17, 28, 43, 50, 51, 52, 55, 56, 57, 58, 62, 63, 66, 68, 72, 85, 98, 104, 105, 106, 121, 125, 126, 129, 130, 138, 142

Cornell, Alex 23

Corporate Communications. . *See* PR

cost per interaction. 112

cost per resolution . . . 109, 110, 111

CRM 38, 53, 58, 77, 81, 122, 123

   and data activation. . . . 124, 125

   and data collection. 124

   and personalization 125, 126, 127

   and technology. 123

Cruise Critic 140

customer advocacy 15, 33, 34, 38, 47, 108, 120

customer experience

   and bots. 131, 132

   and customer expectations . . 18, 19, 130, 143

   and customer service 4, 7, 9, 17, 18, 36, 38, 67, 70, 85, 100, 118

   and feedback loop 117, 119

   and loyalty. 7, 133

   and messaging apps . . . 141, 142

   and personalization 126

   and profitability. 7, 9

   and simplicity . . . 21, 22, 23, 24

   and social media. 3, 16, 17, 18, 19, 38, 142

   and technology. 51, 53, 135

   and user experience 11-15

   definition of. 1-3

   digital. 3, 4, 11

   examples 8, 9, 10

   measurement of 6, 7

   offline 16, 17, 20, 114, 115

   vs. price 5, 6

Customer Experience Index (Forrester) 7

customer loyalty 1, 6, 7, 36, 93, 133

customer satisfaction 1, 69, 79, 106, 109, 129, 142

Customer Service

   and artificial intelligence . . . 80, 131-135

   and CRM. . . . . *See* CRM

   and customer expectations . . 99, 107, 134

   and customer experience . . 4, 7, 9, 17, 18, 36, 38, 67, 70, 85, 100, 118

   and feedback . . . 6, 19, 116-120

   and Marketing 20, 30, 33, 43, 44, 50, 51, 54, 55, 58, 66, 67, 68, 99, 107, 115

   and messaging apps . . . 128-135

and social media. 16, 18, 19, 20, 27-34, 43, 44, 50, 61, 64, 72, 78, 79, 81, 84, 98, 110, 141, 142

as "the new Marketing" 33, 36, 108, 109

examples 25, 31, 33-37, 89-93, 119, 126-127

hiring agents . . . .*See* Team Selection

in the business of 4, 5

proactive 100, 101

public. 19, 20, 29, 30, 31, 32, 36, 38, 60, 63, 81, 82, 87, 91, 104, 108, 118, 128, 129, 142

reporting 103-113

technology 49-56, 58

the future of. 141-143

the marketing of. 142

training agents 72-82

Customer Service on Twitter
Playbook 79, 111

Degnan, James 62

Dell 64, 65, 94, 99, 138

Delta Airlines 30, 99, 100, 142

DiJulius, John R. III. 6, 16, 60, 62, 92, 94, 118

direct message 42, 79, 85, 106, 109, 128

disclosure (legal) 22, 23

Discover Card 33, 34, 36, 42, 43, 57, 74, 87, 93, 142

Do Simple Better 21-24, 26

Duke Energy 69, 70, 93, 101

Edison Research 32, 45, 97

Edmunds 140

email 23, 28, 29, 32, 47, 60, 63, 67, 85, 86, 104, 106, 109, 110, 118, 122, 123, 125, 129, 130, 133, 142, 143

empowering (agents) . . . 44, 52, 78, 92-95,

Facebook 16, 24, 27-30, 42, 43, 44, 51-54, 60, 61, 68, 78, 79, 80, 85, 88, 89, 91, 95, 97, 98, 99, 107, 108, 109, 112, 123, 128, 129, 134, 138, 139, 140, 142

Facebook Messenger. 79, 80, 85, 122, 128, 129

feedback loop 116-120

Fitbit 68, 86, 118, 119, 136, 137, 138, 142

Focus on Customer Service . . . 18, 34, 65, 68, 92, 109, 119, 122, 132

Foresee 109

Forrester. 6, 7, 8

Fulghum, Robert 74

Google 21, 29, 75, 117, 124

Android 3

Let Me Google That For You . .75

Reviews 139

Guinness Book of World Records . . .62

Hahn, Rob. 41, 50, 63, 70, 83, 105

Hamilton, Monty 17, 41, 42, 48, 57, 77, 78, 85, 126, 127

handling time 106

hashtag 26, 54, 60, 61, 129

Health Insurance Portability and Accountability Act of 1996 (HIPAA) 87

hiring . . . . *See* Team Selection

Hootsuite 54

HP Inc. 79

HR 88

Huang, Wayne 45, 46

Hug Your Haters 32, 81, 96, 118

Human Resources . . . . *See* HR

Hyatt 25, 26, 36, 37, 43, 83

Hyken, Shep 5, 17, 30, 44, 65, 71, 74, 83, 87, 94, 95, 120, 126, 132, 134, 140

"I'm On Hold" (song) 22-23

iflix 23

Instagram . . . 30, 44, 51, 61, 78, 112

intelligence augmentation (IA) 132-133

International Organization for Standardization 11

Intuit 136, 139

iOgrapher 97

IVR 28, 47, 50, 52, 131, 132, 134

J.D. Power 6

"jack of all trades" (agents) . . . 47, 72

Jack Threads 31, 95

Jeopardy! 132

JetBlue 45, 63, 93

Kapoor, Kriti 79

Kerpen, Dave 32

Kestens, Davy . . . 30, 43, 49, 50, 51, 66, 80, 104, 122, 128, 130, 131, 132, 141

Kramer, Bryan 32

languages 43, 52

Leahy, Allison 68, 86, 118, 119, 120, 136, 137, 138, 142

Lemin, Daniel 140

Likeable Media 32

LinkedIn 44, 51, 78, 128, 139

Lithium 56

loyalty
　to a brand . . 1, 6, 7, 36, 93, 133
　programs 53, 57, 124

Maddon, Joe 21

Manipurated 140

March, Joshua 17, 43, 44, 50, 55, 66, 121, 129, 130, 132, 133, 138, 142

Mashable 31

Mattson, Michelle 18, 20, 51, 60, 74, 80, 85, 95, 96, 97, 105

Meacham, Laurie 45, 63

messaging apps 51, 70, 78-79, 128-135, 141

Millennials 28, 112, 143

Miller, Nicole 47-48

ModCloth 94

Moriarty, Dan 43, 83

msg.ai 128, 133, 134

National Labor Relations Board
(NLRB) 88
New Voice Media. 5
Nordstrom 74
Obee, Mark 139
Opinion Lab 109
OtterBox 119
Percolate. 54
Periscope 78
personalization 125-127
Personally Identifiable Information
(PII). 86
Philosophy . . . 38, 40-48, 53, 56, 72
   examples 47-48
Piercy, Madeleine . . .69, 70, 93, 101
pinball 125
Pineau-Boddison, Sandra 91
Pinterest. 44, 51, 78, 128
PR 56, 63, 69, 88, 104, 107
Prioritization (of messages). 56,
   57, 67, 97, 98
Process 44, 78, 83-102, 105,
   118, 129, 132
   competitor mentions 101
   indirect mentions. 100
   industry mentions 101
   reactive alerts 100
   recognizing milestones 101
Product Development (team) . . 115,
   119
Protected Health Information
(PHI). 86, 87
Public Relations . . . . .See PR

QQ Mobile 79, 128
questions
   most frequent. 75, 76
   responding to. . . 41, 45, 47, 48,
      117, 133, 138, 139, 141
QuickBooks 139
ratings and reviews 6, 139-140
regulated industry 44, 85, 95
Reporting. 103-113
   agent performance 106
   channel performance . . 107-108
   competitive analysis . . . 112-113
   cost per resolution 109-112
   mentions 104
   post-service engagement. . . 108-
      109
   resolution time. 106
   response time 105
   satisfaction scores 109
   sentiment. 108
   team/center performance . . 106-
      107
   time-based performance. . . .107
   top issues 112
   volume. 104
Residence Inn. 36, 37, 125
resolution time. 46, 67, 106
response rate. 112-113
response time . . . 32, 44, 45, 48, 67,
   97-98, 105, 106, 107, 108, 109,
   112, 113, 130
Rule of Reply Only Twice. . . . 96-97
Salesforce 54, 123

Scotty's Brewhouse 4, 18, 19, 26, 30, 40, 64, 94, 117, 140

sentiment 6, 46, 57, 108

SEO .138

Service Aptitude 60, 94

Snapchat 44, 78, 128, 129

social media

   and customer experience 3, 16, 17, 18, 19, 38, 142

   and Customer Service 16, 18, 19, 20, 27-34, 43, 44, 50, 61, 64, 72, 78, 79, 81, 84, 98, 110, 141, 142

   differences from other channels 28, 29, 30, 34, 72, 104, 109, 111, 118

   listening 6, 27, 28, 37, 68, 100, 101, 116-117, 119, 137

   platforms 27, 43-44, 49, 51-52, 53, 78-80

   sharing on . . . 17, 36, 78, 82, 99

Social Media Marketing World 25-26

Southwest Airlines . . 41, 50, 63, 70, 83, 105

Sparkcentral 29, 30, 43, 49, 51, 56, 66, 67, 70, 80, 81, 94, 104, 109, 123, 128, 141

Spotify 34-36, 92

Spredfast 54

Sprinklr 54

Sprint 129

Sprout Social 54, 80, 104, 112-113

Statista 128

surprise and delight 25-26, 30, 36-38, 92-93, 95, 125

SurveyMonkey 109

Team Selection 59-71

   Customer Service vs. social media skills 61-62

   emotional intelligence . . . 64-65

   job description 60

   writing skills 60-61

Technology providers 49-58

   all-in-one 51, 54

   collision avoidance 56

   contract 58

   dedicated service provider . . 51, 54-56

   free/mass subscriptions . . . 53-54

   innovation roadmap 53

   integration with CRM 58

   integration with social platforms 51, 52

   investment 51

   language support 52

   prioritization 56-57

   reporting 57

   security 57-58

   speed to market 58

   strategic support 53

   technical support 52-53

   workflow options 52

telephone (channel) 28, 29, 47, 60, 67, 69-70, 85, 123, 141, 143

Telstra 17, 41, 42, 48, 57, 77, 78, 85, 122, 126, 127

The Customer Service Revolution . . 6, 16, 62, 92, 94, 118

The Definitive Guide to Social, Mobile Customer Service 17, 28, 51, 52, 55, 57, 58, 62, 63, 68, 72, 85, 98, 104, 105, 106, 125, 126, 130

There is no B2B or B2C It's Human to Human: #H2H 32

Thomas, Sam 34

T-Mobile 18, 20, 51, 60, 74, 80, 85, 95, 101, 105

Today Show, The 31

Training 72-82

    approval status 82

    brand voice 74

    community management . . 80-81

    frequently asked questions . 75-76

    known irritants 76

    other areas of the business . . . 73

    policies 77-78

    social media platforms . . . 78-80

TripAdvisor 140

trolls 96-97

Tull, David 31, 95

Tung, Eric 25, 26, 36, 37, 125

Turbo Tax 136

TweetDeck 54

Twitter 16, 18, 26-30, 37, 42-46, 50-54, 60, 61, 62, 78, 79, 85, 89, 90, 91, 97, 99, 100, 105-109, 111, 112, 126, 128, 138, 140, 141, 142

    handles 99-100, 126, 138

    research 18, 45, 46, 79

Uber 14-15

United Airlines 89-92

user experience 11-15

Vega 92-93, 119

Voice of the Customer 6, 115-116, 122

Watson (IBM) 132-133

WeChat 44, 51, 79, 128

Wendy's 8-9

What's The Secret?: To Providing a World-Class Customer Experience 60

WhatsApp . . . 51, 79, 128, 129, 131

Whole Foods Market 47

Wise, Scott 4, 5, 9, 18, 19, 26, 30, 40, 41, 64, 65, 74, 94, 117, 118, 140

"Wow" Moment 25-26, 36-37

Xbox 62

Yahoo 21

Yelp 139, 140

YouTube 23, 79

Zappos 115

About the Author

Dan Gingiss has focused on consistently delighting customers throughout a 20-year career spanning multiple disciplines including marketing, customer service, social media, and digital customer experience. He hosts the Focus on Customer Service podcast, interviewing leaders at brands which are renowned for outstanding customer service in social media.

Gingiss was named one of the "30 Most Influential People in Social Customer Service" by Conversocial, one of the "Top 15 NPS and Customer Service Thought Leaders to Follow in 2017" by CustomerGauge, one of the "Top 10 Service Cloud Influencers" by Traackr, and one of "30 Influencers That Drive Social Media for the Brands We Love" by Leadtail and Purematter.

Gingiss holds a B.A. in psychology and communications from the University of Pennsylvania, and an M.B.A. in marketing and strategy from the Kellogg School of Management at Northwestern University. He currently resides in Chicago. Follow him on Twitter at @dgingiss or visit his website at www.winningatsocial.com.

Made in the USA
Columbia, SC
16 June 2017